FRINTON PAST

The Cliff Road, Frinton, 1920 (postcard loaned by Mr M Herbert)

FRINTON PAST

Stan Jarvis

Ian Henry Publications

ISBN 0 86025 494 1

Published by
Ian Henry Publications, Ltd.
20 Park Drive, Romford, Essex RM1 4LH
and printed by
Interprint, Ltd.
Industrial Estate, Marsa HMR 15, Malta

ACKNOWLEDGEMENTS

A book attempting to cover over two thousand years of the story of an Essex town could not be written without the help of a host of interested and generous people, Frinton friends too numerous to mention. Without them this book could not have been so well illustrated.

I thank my publisher for his support down the years in the production of other books on the fair county of Essex.

Above all I am grateful to Hazel, my wife, for her ever-ready help and encouragement in what has been a long and fascinating task.

John Norden's map of Essex, 1594

STAN JARVIS

The Greensward, 1905 (Chelmsford Library)

FOREWORD

Frinton is to many people a 'special' place. Special not only to those who live there, for all round Essex and further afield I frequently meet people with very happy memories of Frinton in childhood or as parents - the beach, the beach huts, on day trips or holiday home stays. They remember above all its unspoilt, uncommercial, natural charm, the perfect place for family holidays. People move to Frinton for those very qualities. It is not better than anywhere else, superficially it is similar to many other small seaside towns, but the combination of tree-lined avenues, Edwardian family homes, old-fashioned shops, a sunny climate, and one of the loveliest and safest beaches in England, together with absence of piers, amusement arcades and commercialisation has great appeal. These attractions have survived for 100 years but not without determined efforts by those who enjoy them, who are happy to share them but not to surrender them. Frinton's defenders fear that the changes sought by some, often newcomers or non-residents, would alter the character of the town for the worse; attempts to impose such changes continue all the time but the 'fierce independence' noted in 1950, albeit mellowed a little, is still able to assert itself.

Change is of course inevitable. New housing developments around Frinton, especially 'outside the Gates', have made new Frinton (2167 voters in December, 1998) approach the size of old Frinton (3176 voters) which, as Stan Jarvis shows, is itself only some 100 years old. As a former Chairman of the Frinton Primary School Governors, I realised that some of the youngest children might well live into the 22nd Century. Some of the enormous changes in the first hundred years are described in this book; who can even guess what these children will look back on in a hundred years time.

The early history of a tiny hamlet - dark ages, Domesday, mediæval - is meticulously documented by Stan Jarvis, reflecting particularly the story of the old Church, the lordship of the manor and the few residents down the years. But the fascination of Frinton as a town lies in its very rapid transformation after the coming of the railway station in 1888 and the rescue and completion by Sir Richard Cooper of the gracious development planned by the Marine and General Land Company at the end of the Nineteenth Century. The growth in number of residents, houses, churches, shops, famous visitors, hotels and leisure amenities is vividly chronicled. The lively era between the two World Wars, the Twenties and Thirties, is brought to life through the writings and reminiscences of those who lived through the period.

Interestingly, many issues which generate heated discussion in our time had the same effect years ago - such as a bus service in Frinton (1934), dog-fouling (1934), parking of cars on the Esplanade (1936), storm damage to beach huts, particularly the Walings (1938); indeed there are many reminders that the sea can be an enemy.

Enjoying as I do the attractions and the pace and way of life in Frinton, I read Stan Jarvis' book with great interest and pleasure. It will introduce the 'special' nature of the town to those who do not know it and to those who might seek to change it. As for me, it enhanced my enjoyment of the town as, I am sure, it will for many other lovers of Frinton.
April, 1999

David Rex
COUNTY COUNCILLOR FOR FRINTON AND WALTON
CURRENTLY CHAIRMAN OF ESSEX COUNTY COUNCIL
SOMETIME CHAIRMAN OF FRINTON AND WALTON TOWN COUNCIL

CHAPTER ONE

It is impossible to write accurately of the origin of Frinton as a human settlement. The fields in which earliest members of the human race wandered in search of food and water have been washed away by the ocean's relentless pounding through countless ages. Miller Christy, in *Durrant's Handbook for Essex*, published in 1887, describes Frinton as "A small parish the greater portion of which has been washed away by the waves, the site of its Hall being now half a mile out to sea."

The geology of this parish is basic; the thick covering of London Clay, which we might call the counterpane on the bed of Essex, can be 25 feet thick or more, as seen where it is exposed clearly to the eye in the cliffs of Frinton and Walton. This heavy clay yields no fossils, but it does contain strange nodules of 'argillaceous limestone' - in other words lumps of really hard, compacted clay known popularly as 'cement-stones', or septaria, of which says the *Oxford English Dictionary,* "parts near the centre are cracked, the spaces being filled with some mineral, formerly much used for cement." We shall see later how they became the subject of a flourishing local industry on the coast from Clacton and Frinton up to Harwich.

The geology section of the *Victoria History of Essex*, published in 1903, gives the best explanation: "The cracks or septa are filled with calc-spar, and sometimes contain pyrites or 'copperas'. The septaria no doubt originated from the segregation of the more calcareous portions of the clayey mud after the deposition of the London Clay." The stiff and sticky London Clay was known by the locals right down to recent times as 'platimore'. A rare covering of the London Clay was noticed by William Whitaker in 1877: "At the top of the cliffs at Frinton there was, in 1871, a short section showing a few feet of light-coloured, false-bedded sand, with a very little gravel scattered through it. On the S.E. of this there were also gravelly patches along the cliff top ... over the London Clay and often capped by a clayey soil. These patches are quite unmappable." Further erosion has taken away this interesting geological stratum.

Frinton gets a mention in that important land utilisation survey called *The Land of Britain* published in 1942, where it says: "The Clacton plain differs somewhat from the other two areas because only a relatively small area is brick-earth. There are patches of gravel at Brightlingsea, Thorpe-le-Soken and Walton-on-the-Naze; the chief soil, however, is medium London Clay. In the main, cultivation is on the light soils and pasture on the clay. It is probable that market gardening would be of no importance were it not for the great numbers of people who visit Clacton, Frinton and Walton during the summer." A well bored at a maltings at Thorpe-le-Soken in 1876, under the supervision of Peter Bruff, chief engineer of the Tendring Hundred Waterworks Company, started at

35 feet above low water mark, went through some 130 feet of London Clay, or Platimore, then 60 feet of Reading Beds (clay and sand) to reach a stratum of chalk which extended on down to 370 feet, when water was at last found. In a short time that water rose to within 20 feet of the surface. Bruff's appearance on the Frinton scene, like a *deus ex machina* at the end of the nineteenth century is recounted later.

Bearing in mind that erosion has taken away the best part of the ancient settlement of Frinton, we could reasonably assume that the London Clay was the begetter of the grassland on which those hardy Ancient Britons hunted their food, farmed primitively and raised their families. The tools of Stone Age man have been found at Clacton, and here at Frinton implements and weapons of flint have been found on the beach at various times, to show that man was here when the land stretched so much further out to sea some forty to fifty thousand years ago. Further evidence of human activity at this time and in this area is shown in the 'Red Hills' which have been identified at Kirby Quay and on the Naze before further erosion.

These were the places where early man fashioned long wide clay dishes, piled them with brushwood and forest litter, filled the with sea water and lit the bonfire to heat the dishes and boil away the seawater entirely so that they could collect the residue of salt. Salt was the gold of those ancient civilisations; it was carried far inland in trading for tools and weapons, hides and hunting dogs.

Life flowed on in Frinton. The Romans came to Essex in 43 A.D., built their *Colonia* at Colchester, survived the Boudican revolt of 62, and Frinton simply carried on in its old ways. Travellers brought their tales however and one or two brave souls went to see the amazing buildings and the noisy market place at Colchester. By the later days of Roman rule (they had gone by the end of the fifth century) Frinton had been drawn into the ways of the new civilisation. Evidence comes in the form of some broken bits of Roman-British pottery found at the seaward end of Connaught Avenue where a silted up ditch marked a field boundary of the time. The *Victoria History* of our county reported in 1963, the finding in Fourth Avenue: "In and after 1904 a trench, filled with black earth containing Romano-British potsherds, was observed in the cliff-edge nearly opposite Connaught Avenue. It was seen again about 1910, during alterations to Kelvin Lodge, Fourth Avenue. This line running WSW coincides with a former farm hedge-bank which can still be traced in the greensward and in private gardens on the west of Fourth Avenue." Two Roman coins have also been found, one on the beach and the other somewhere in the general area of Frinton.

That is the extent of the Roman occupation of Frinton as it can be traced today. We leave the Romano-British living their quiet lives for at least a couple of centuries until the Saxon seafarers who had raided the coast in summer forays across the North Sea decided that what we now call Essex was a fair place for permanent settlement. The brooding, tenantless Roman-built 'Forts of the Saxon Shore' no longer frightened them off. One extended family clan, looking to a leader called Fritha - probably a shortened form of his name, came ashore at this place, found a gap in the cliffs, climbed up to take a look inland and liked what they saw. They settled, built their wooden longhouse or Hall, and let it be known to the flow of following settlers that this patch already taken, settled as a 'ton' by Fritha's people. So it was that this geographical location first became identified as Frinton. The Saxon settlement slowly spread inland, but no evidence in building or in artifact - other than the possibility of some late Saxon stonework in the nave of the old church - has survived to support the theory of the origin of the place name and the evolution of Frinton.

The date of the building of the settlement's first church is quite unknown. It is generally thought that the conversion of the Saxons in Essex to Christianity began in the middle of the seventh century and spread rapidly throughout the county. Fritha's people would have acquiesced to his wishes in the matter of this new religion, and after discussion amongst the warriors in Fritha's Hall a suitable site would have been selected and the building of a church would have been put in hand. It is most likely that it would have been a timber construction, using trees growing in the area and cut down on the spot.

So hundreds of years of history pass by in mists of time quite impenetrable. In about 1047 the Anglo-Saxon Chronicle reported that Walton-on-the-Naze was the scene of a minor naval invasion 'by that outlawed Danish pirate Osgood dapa and his men'. It is due to another invasion that we at last derive some details of this place called Frinton, or Frietuna, or Frientunam as it is written in the Domesday Book. That 'Book', as everybody knows, was gradually compiled over several years before its completion and submission to William the Conqueror in 1086. There are two entries for this tiny settlement, showing that even by such an early date this Saxon estate had been divided into two portions. An English translation of these entries in the official Latin of the time reads:

"Hundred of Tendring ...

Frietuna, which was held by Harold, in King Edward's time, as a manor and three hides [measurement of area] was afterwards held by Ingelric, is now held of the count by Ralf de Marci. [Population was] then 6 villeins; now. Then 3 bordars; now none. Then 2 serfs; now 1. Then, as now, one plough on the demesne [the lord's personal estate]. Then 2 ploughs belonging to the villagers, now they have but one to share. There is enough pasture to keep 60 sheep. [but there are at present]20 sheep, 2 beasts and 7 swine. It was then worth [in revenue to the crown] 60 shillings; now £4 and ten shillings."

The second entry shows that in the same Hundred of Tendring:

"Frientuna, which was held by Levesun, as a manor and 3½ hides, is held of Geoffrey [de Mandeville] by Renelm [or Rainald]. Then and afterwards 3 villeins; now 1. Then and afterwards 4 serfs; now 3. Then as now 2 ploughs on the demesne. There were 2 ploughs belonging to the men, now only a half. 312 acres of meadow with pasture for 50 sheep. Then there were 49 sheep, now 40 and 2 rounceys and swine. It was then worth £7, now £4."

This is only the roughest translation, a full explanation of the entries and the terms used will be found in Volume One of the *Victoria History of the County of Essex*. One term it is necessary to explain here is the use of 'then' and 'now'. 'Then' was in the time of Edward the Confessor, the last Anglo-Saxon king of the old line, who died in 1066, and 'now' is the very time at which William the Conqueror's clerks were riding through the land compiling this great inventory of the country's assets and its payments into the new king's coffers.

So we see that at some time after the Saxon settlement when 'Fritha was the head of his clan and administered its government from his hall, some circumstance caused a division of the land. A précis showing the descent of manor of Frinton from 1198 down to 1819, prepared by C W Hayne in 1938 helps to clear the picture. The main manor, the 'overlordship' of Frinton, previous to 1198 by Ralph Fitz Richard was inherited by two sisters, Amy and Sarah, widows respectively of Oger Fitz Oger and Michael Fitz Oger, who were brothers. In their share of the property Amy was assigned the "Knight's Fee in Frinton" which the Domesday Book quotes as being held of Geoffrey de Mandeville. The lesser manor was held as a quarter of a knight's fee, which meant that the tenant was obliged to provide one quarter of the cost of providing a knight to fight for the King in time of war. It was the subject of a similar partition between two heirs, the Tregoz sisters. One, Agnes, married Geoffrey de Norford; the other, Petronilla, was the wife of Ralph Travers. After due negotiation, as shown in the court record of the time, the 'Feet of Fine' Agnes was assigned the ownership; "... unless perchance Ralph should have an heir by Petronilla, [in which case] all the said lands shall be divided between the two sisters or their heirs ... " These names crop up again in 1205-6, during King John's reign when Geoffrey de Norford ceded to Petronilla Tregoz "100s. of land with appurtenances in Frienton" for "20 marks of silver" - a value quite impossible to translate into modern money.

The *Oxford English Dictionary* defines the mark thus: "In England, after the Conquest, the ratio of 20 sterling pennies to an ounce was the basis of computation; hence the value of the mark became fixed at 160 pence = 13s 4d, or ⅔ of the £ sterling."

The way of life of the ordinary folk of Frinton carried on in rhythm with the seasons, working the land in accordance with their station on the manor, from the Lord's steward through the farmer tenants, the peasants on their own strips of land, as well as their obligations of labour for the lord; and serfs who were bound inextricably in service to the lord - to live or die at his whim. We have no record of their coming and going but some pin points of light shine out from the darkness of history concerning the manor and the church.

In 1199 the owners of the two manors went to court to determine which of them had the right to appoint the priest of the parish. This was of greater importance than we realise today and gave pecuniary and political advantage. The King's Court decided Richard Fitzralph, probably the son of Ralph, had the right to present the priest because his father had actually presented the last incumbent some seven years before. So Geoffrey de Norford, of the smaller manor, was the loser. National records show the manors being leased from the great landed owners by various tenants hoping to make a living from the land. During the thirteenth century the De Burnhams, the de Leyes and John Fitz Bernard were some of the tenants, while the ownership ran through the Trickets, Humhrey Bohun and Walter le Gros. The last-named family was still there in 1346 and de Burnhams turn up again in a record of 1356. It was in 1230 when Henry III was on the throne that Stephen de Plesingho (the ancient name for Willingale Doe) sold to William de Burnham "one knight's fee with appurtenances in Frinton" for the consideration of 20 marks.

What of the settlement itself at this time? P B Boyden, in *Frinton before the Stuarts* (1978) tells us: "Frinton in the 1230's was clearly a very small place - its total extent was probably not more than 600 acres, and its assessment in the 1237-8 Subsidy [a special tax] was only 8/- out of a total of £25/4/9 for the Tendring Hundred (excluding the Sokens). Two other places only contributed less than Frinton, whilst Little Holland's assessment was 12/-."

We have seen how the Lordship of the two manors of Frinton had already been ceded to families not resident in the Manor House. The parish did not even have a resident rector or a vicar appointed by him to serve the parish. By around 1250, however, an unidentified 'Walter' is shown on the list of rectors kept in the church. By 1280 or thereabouts one 'Geoffrey' is named as the Rector.

It was a national enquiry which next brought news of Frinton at this time. Edward I was vigorous in introducing the groundwork of our country's statute law, advised by the greatest lawyers of the age. He set in motion over two years from 1274 the enquiry called the Quo Warranto inquest which demanded of owners of property and holders of privileges by what authority they had power to enjoy these lands and payments. The commissioners sent out to hear the claims produced a record of their findings written painstakingly in ink on sheets of parchment. These sheets were arranged under the 'Hundreds' or groups of parishes into which the counties were divided for administrative purposes.

Frinton gets two entries. First, it was found by the enquiry that the Dean and Chapter of St. Paul's, in whom Frinton's church was vested from Saxon times, had usurped the rights of the crown in taking goods as sureties in certain abstruse court cases, but, more than that, they had also claimed their right to all the wrecked ships and the goods they contained, washed ashore under Frinton's cliffs. Since the commissioners were not shown any evidence of the church's right to these 'perks' they were cancelled forthwith. Yet, in 1303 the church was still claiming the right to salvage goods from a ship wrecked on the sands.

The second entry reveals that a certain Walter of Tillingham, a bailiff or local government officer, of Colchester went over to Frinton to supervise a meeting of the leaders of the community there. Because one of them did not turn up Walter charged that meeting one mark - then equal to 13s 4d. - and pocketed it himself! It was obviously time that King Edward tightened up on his revenue accounts.

We can follow up the devolution of the ownership of the manors through that account by C W Hayne. In 1348, the twenty-second year of the reign of Edward III, John de Burnham had to sue Geoffrey de Ruly and his wife Eleanor to preserve his right of presentation of the minister to the Church of Frinton. Eight years later that man gets another mention in our national records, this time the Miscellaneous Papers of the Exchequer, because he took away a cask of wine that had been washed up on the shore, when such flotsam was rightly the property of the monarch. A similar incident occurred in 1398 when "William Godmanston of Frynton was fined for taking a Whale cast upon the sand in the hundred of Tendring without licence."

It was Godmanston who, in 1428, was holding the manor of 'a ¼ of a Knight's Fee' in Frinton formerly held by John de Burnham. In 1446 John Godmanston bought half the larger manor from J Dovewood and Geoffrey Rokell. By 1476, however, it is recorded in the Patent Roll of 28th May that the manor of 'Frempton' was granted to Sir Robert Chamberleyn.

But we must get our heads out of those dusty old manuscripts and look at the place itself for evidence of a great happening in Frinton a hundred years before Sir Robert was lord of all he surveyed. The happening was the rebuilding of the old church which, as far as we can trace, had always been in the possession of the Dean and Chapter of St. Paul's Cathedral, to whom profits from rent of its land and tithes from the parishioners would have been paid. But was this new church on the same site as that first timber church the Saxons built?

The extent of erosion and the enforced change of site for the new church can be gauged from the fact that the old St. Mary's was estimated to be 300 yards from the cliff edge in 1863. By the time the cliffs had been graded behind their concrete sea defences in 1906 the distance was reduced to more or less 160 yards. In 1879 when restoration of that new (now old) church laid bare the foundations of its chancel, it was discovered that it had been built on a bed of shingle brought up from the beach, and neither limed or cemented. There was no archaeological evidence of any previous building or of man's occupation of this site.

No actual date for the building of this church has been established, the county histories concerning themselves only with the almost total rebuilding and restoration of 1879, so we must go back to the Hall, the manor house, its owners and occupiers. We know Sir Robert Chamberleyn was Lord of the Manor by 1476, but we can fill in quite a gap before this date, though it must be said that there were purchases and leases through the previous century of which not sufficient record has survived to enable us to make more than a guess at the true descent of those two old manors.

By 1392 the owner of the Manor of Frinton was the Duke of Gloucester, Thomas of Woodstock, with John Rokell tenant, including also the smaller manor representing a quarter of a knight's fee'. The Peasants' Revolt of 1381 which involved large numbers of Essex men seems to have had little effect on Frinton and its tiny population.

While there was a sale of land at Frinton on quite a large scale in 1423 we know that the Rokells retained the Lordship and the Manor House as a Geoffrey Rokell was still patron of the living in 1426 when he chose Thomas Barry as Rector, It was a strange time for the church and its little congregation; Barry was there just a couple of months, to be succeeded on 9th December by Richard Selby who was at the same time Rector of Bradwell-on-Sea. In just another two months he was gone, to be replaced by John Stony on 14th February, 1427.

The tenancy of the chief manor, under the overlordship of the great Bourchier family, passed to the Godmanston family who bought it from the Rokells by instalments over five years. The priest appointed by the Rokells continued until his death in 1435 or thereabouts, when John Toby was appointed by the Godmanstons. Three more rectors followed down to 1473. William Godmanston had died in supporting his king at the Battle of Barnet in 1471, so it was his widow Joanna who presented Henry Fitton to the living as rector in 1473.

Then there was a strange hiccup in the Godmanston saga. Peter Boyden in *Frinton before the Stuarts*, explains: "The new regime of Edward IV confiscated all the Godmanston estates and granted them to Sir Robert Chamberleyn, the king's servant, in May, 1475. So it was that Sir Robert presented (in January, 1476) the next rector, Geoffrey Hynd, Priest, on Fitton's resignation which occurred late in 1475. The Godmanston estates were subsequently restored to the family..." Joanna married again, to Sir Gilbert Hussey and she continued to appoint the priest in 1493 and 1495. When Joanna died her interest in the Manor passed to her first husband's sister, Phillipa Godmanston.

So the fifteenth century passes in Frinton, with the curtain of history hardly drawn back on the life of the ordinary people of the time. Since even as late as 1861 the Census records the population of Frinton as just 29 souls there would have little to report on in the daily routine when Adam was delving and Eve was spinning in the age-old cycle of life linked to the seasons and the festivals and fasts of the Church calendar.

Harbottle Grimston's indenture

This Indenture

In the opening years of the sixteenth century Phillipa Godmanston married Henry Walker and they had a daughter named Christiana. She married William Brown and they get mentioned in the written record of the Frinton story when, as Lord and Lady of the Manor, they) appointed the next Rector, Richard Whitmore, in February, 1533. His reign was brief; he died in 1542. By that time William Brown had also died and Christiana re-married, to Humphrey Dymock. They appointed the new minister, John Hanmere, in October, 1542. Then there is a mystery, for when this rector died his successor, John Leke, was chosen by Sir Francis Cockaine, and this man's qualification for having the right of 'presentment' cannot now be established.

It is in 1532 that the name 'Skirman's Fee' is added to the title of the Manor of Frinton Hall. The descent of the Manor is taken a step further by the grant in April, 1543, which records that Isabella Brown leased the "Waters, Weirs, Fisheries, etc." to John Moreton at £20 per annum, during the life of Christiana, widow of William Brown and now wife of Humphrey Dymock. It would appear from a Charter in the British Museum dated 4th May 1544 that within a year John Moreton was leasing the whole of the Manor. By 6th October, 1610, we have it from a Chancery Inquisition that Edward Grimston of Bradfield who had bought the Manor in 1603, had died recently in possession of what is termed "The Manor of Skirmans Fee otherwise Frinton Hall. The next available document, of 10th March, 1628, in terms of the old calendar, shows in a Grimston family marriage settlement that their possessions include "The manors of Frinton and Skirman's Fee." Here we come up against a tricky problem, for in a manorial court of 4th April "in the 38th year of Elizabeth's reign" (i.e. 1596) Skyrman's Fee is declared to be in 'Clacton Magna' and on 6th September, 1613, the lands belonging to Skyrman's Fee are recorded as being in 'Clacton Magna & Clacton Parva & Frinton'. After that the actual court book simply shows it as the "Court of Harbottel Grimeston, Milit. et Barronet." (Knight and Baronet). Yet in 1616 for some special reason not explained in existing documents, the Rector of Frinton was appointed by no less a person that King James I himself.

The difficulty of describing the doings of the tiny hamlet of Frinton at this time has been put so well by Peter Boyden in *Frinton before the Stuarts*: "Of those lower down the social scale who tilled the land, minded the sheep, and produced the few pounds which constituted the cash benefits of being the owner of Frinton, precious little has been said for the simple reason that there is hardly any source other than Domesday which mentions them."

This small place on the breezy cliffs was self sufficient in its agriculture and its handicrafts and minded its own business, but there are just one or two side-lights on life in Frinton to be gained from the assize court records of those days, now carefully preserved in the Essex Record Office. A sad sidelight indeed is the case of the servant woman who worked for Henry Mopted, a yeoman farmer of Frinton. She became pregnant - was he the father? - she kept her secret. When she went into labour she delivered the baby herself, then, the prosecution claimed, she threw it to her pigs. But at the trial the jury took the view that, as she had claimed, the baby had been stillborn and that her only crime was in not sending for the midwife and having expert attention. The outcome of this tragic episode will never be known because the record of the judgment itself no longer exists.

A much less dramatic case which came before the Assize Court, meeting in Chelmsford on 7th July, 1669, shows that James Baker of "Frenton" had been brought to court by Robert Baker - probably his son or a near relation - because he had refused to pay the wages due to him. The entry in the record is of the briefest, but there is a note added by the Justice: "The wages before me was proved £1.13s.0d." While his man had worked hard for his money and had been denied it there was another case tried on 14th July 1691 concerning two men who did not even try to get a job. It was stated that "Abraham Walters of Tendring and Thomas Porter of Frinton, labourers, before and since 11 July (the previous year) lived idly out of service." They should have bound themselves to a master and found themselves visible means of support as the law demanded, but there they were scraping a living by poaching, casual work, even thieving, yet in such a tiny community as Frinton they must have stuck out like a sore thumb.

Another strange snippet of Frinton history is gathered from the report on the state of the clergy of Essex in 1604, which states:

"Mr Forthe, a dumbe minister, is parson there, he is also parson of Holland Magna [Great Holland]; he keepeth not anie curate longe together for wante of sufficient allowance, he is also a grazier." Dumb he may have been, business-like he certainly was; while the poor curates took the services of a Sunday Mr. Forthe over at Great Holland was fattening his cattle on the green grasslands - and selling them, at Colchester market, no doubt, at a good profit.

The next remarkable record of Frinton, in the last years of the sixteenth century and the first half of the seventeenth is the original court book of the Manor of Skyrman's Fee, in other words, Frinton Hall. It covers from 1582 to 1641 and is preserved in the Essex Record Office. It must be said that the writing is not readable unless one has both knowledge of Latin and of the old style of handwriting and spelling. The book is made up of paper pages bound in a parchment sheet of a copy of an unidentified deed of contemporary date. We see that when the book begins, on 1st May, 1582, Marie Cockayne, widow, was Lady of the Manor. The list of tenants which also included holders of land now in Clacton and Walton, mentions, tells us the principal inhabitants of that tiny, insignificant hamlet of Frinton. Often the actual people are only referred to as the heirs of the original tenant of the Lord of the Manor. For example:

"The heirs of Barbara Cawston hold land called Deathes" - the name of an early owner long since dead.

"The heirs of John Gover hold land called Blykesland and Byrchins over a lane adjacent."

Thomas Wollmer holds a tenement called Pondhouse and land called Pondhouse lands belonging."

Thomas Porter who occupied land called Hunts and Gogyers, and more in "Marsh End towards Skyrmans Hill", had to include two capons as part of his annual rent. The list concludes with the rent received from "The holder of the land at Marsh End, one formerly William Teye."

By 1627 the Court Book shows the Lord of the Manor as Harbottle Grimston and his steward, or agent, presiding over the court, was Henry Sterling. New names of tenants appear. For example, James Stonehouse had replaced John Gover at Blykeland in Great Clacton and Jeremia Burgess is mentioned as holding land and a tenement called Crispes in Frinton which he had willed to his wife Penelope if she outlived him. The last court recorded, that of 1st October, 1642, does not offer any further information on Frinton.

Many towns and villages can gather much information on their early history from the parish registers of baptisms, marriages and burials. They were introduced by Thomas Cromwell, Vicar-General to Henry VIII, but despite threat of a fine for non-compliance the response was not universal. In Frinton's case we shall never know how assiduous the Rector or his clerk were in keeping these records because all of those kept before 1764 have been inexplicably lost. Richard Stone, indefatigable churchwarden, of whom more later, wrote in one of the existing registers, on 9th June, 1868: "Note of Baptisms for Frinton found in Kirby registers lent by Revd. W L Coxhead, beginning in 1681; in which I find several births - deaths - marriages of persons then resident in the Parish of Frinton down to 1768 - & only sorry the documents & accounts relative to the parish of Frinton, except for a few old pen notes are lost."

It may be that the neglect of the registers went hand in hand with the neglect of the ancient church, for Nikolaus Pevsner, the expert on Essex architecture, places the oldest existing part of that church - the south porch - as of the early sixteenth century. The destructive hand of time was working in another way; its agency the sea. Erosion of the coast was so considerable that any features which might have added to our knowledge of Frinton at this time - tracks and footpaths, early houses, farm buildings - have simply been washed away, Dr T W Hicks, writing *The Story of the Churches of Frinton* in 1938, thought that sea erosion was such a factor in the Frinton story that he devoted a special section to it:

"Standing on our Greensward. Frinton's pride and justifiably so, and looking seawards, it is difficult to conceive that somewhere on that ocean bed are the remains of three dead villages: Walton, Frinton and Holland. As to how populous they were I can find no authentic history; certain it is that one of them possessed a thirteenth century Church, which in 1796 was nearly all gone, and by 1880 had entirely disappeared into the sea. The Eastern Province is of course mainly low lying, 300 feet above sea level is the highest point, great stretches of it are waterways, tidal marshes,or heathland. The gravel soil with chalk ridges trends off to a heavier clay Southward, and it is due to this particular formation that the sea has its devastating effect.

The Parish Church of Frinton (St Mary's) is a vivid example' it stands about 160 yds. from the cliff and, in 1863 it was described as being 300 yards from the cliff. To quote the note of Richard Stone in 1824: "60 rods from Front Door of Frinton Hall to Beach or 55 to edge of Cliff." In 1857 there is a further note: "The sea is encroaching very fast and it would not surprise me if it [*i.e.* the church] has to be moved back before many years." (1862) "The Parish is gradually wasting". (1865) "The sea is still encroaching."

How vast that 'heathland' on which those three villages were, none can tell, but the old sages of Walton still say, that 'out there' in certain settings of the tide the old church bell has been heard to ring and, at extreme low tides, ominous breakers have been seen, significant of the old foundation of the one-time Church."

The Court Book of the Manor of Frinton ends with an account of the proceedings of the meeting on 1st October, 1642, without any further mention of land or people of Frinton. The Manor cannot be said to have been of great value or of any historical significance in the county, let alone national affairs. A list of Lords of the Manor compiled by Frances Bates shows the Grimston family in that seat of power from 1603 down to around 1690. The Warrens took over and stayed there for some 35 years, then it changed hands eight times down to 1850.

The site of the old Manor House is now somewhere out to sea. We know this on more than one authority. The Reverend William Holman was Congregational minister at Halstead from 1700 until his death in 1730. He was an enthusiastic enquirer into the history of the county who, in his time at Halstead, amassed 400 notebooks - one for each parish; travelling assiduously to complete his notes. The book he envisaged was never published but the information he collected passed from hand to hand until it was acquired twenty years after his death by Philip Morant and ordered and absorbed into his famous history, published 1760-68. Holman's information on Frinton can still be seen in his original notebook now kept in the Essex Record Office, headed *The History of Holland Magna et Parva (and Frinton)* by William Holman. We quote the notes in full because they include the interesting information on the fate of the old Frinton Hall:

"This Parish lies on the main sea next to Great Holland; near the Gunfleet; about 58 miles from London. In Domesday 'tis written Frintuna and Fretuna from whence comes the present name of Frinton and was held by Geoffrey de

Magnaville & Eustace Earle of Bulloign. John Norden (the early mapmaker) tells us that in some records 'tis called Frunting, as being on the very Front or Brow of the sea cliffe [then a page has been removed] ... Hence only the mannor of Frinton called Skurmans Fee alias Frinton Hall. The Mansion House is scituated upon the Beach..."

As to the Manor, we do get another glimpse of light when Edward Alston first approached Sir Harbottle Grimston concerning the purchase of "The Manor of Frinton and the Manor Seigniory of Skirman's Fee together with wrecks of the sea." By 1661 Alston, now knighted, was selling "The manors of Frinton alias Frinton Hall and Skirman's Fee to his brother Pennings Alston. At the end of the century a court case of 1695 concerning who was entitled to the tithes of Frinton Hall showed that Thomas Warren was then the owner of, and had lived in the Hall, and after he died his widow Elizabeth continued to live there.

An interesting connection with this Lord of the manor is made by Gurney Benham, Mayor of Colchester three times between 1892 and 1934, in his book, *Essex Sokens*, which is worth quoting in full:

"About Captain James Bushell, who "fished for wrecks" [a quote from Morant's *History* of 1768] I have found rather more information ... I assume he is identical with James Bushell, mariner, of Little Holland, who married Joan, daughter of Thomas Warren, mariner, of Wapping, who was lord of the manor of Frinton in 1691. His son, Jeremiah Warren, 'gentleman', who succeeded him at Frinton, was made a free burgess of Colchester in 1729.

Captain James Bushell was born in 1673, and, according to the *London Magazine* (Vol.7, p. 361), died on July 3, 1738, in his 66th year. He was "very expert in the art of diving," says the magazine.

There are further particulars in the *London Evening Post* of July 11 - 13, 1738, which states that he died, "as he was at work on the wreck that lately happened in the Middle Swin on the coast of Essex." The Middle Swin, is about twenty miles S.E. of Frinton. "He made a hearty dinner," we are told, "and within an hour after died, as 'tis thought, of a fit of the cholick."

He was five feet eleven inches high and six feet round the belly, very skilful in the art of diving, which he followed near forty years. One would like to know more of him and his diving achievements. Diving in those days was a dangerous and unscientific business. Divers wore a 'watertight leather case', which held about half a hogshead (some 25 gallons) of air, and was so adapted as to give free play to the arms and legs, so that the wearer could walk on the sea bottom, examine a sunken vessel and salve her cargo, returning to the surface when his supply of air was getting exhausted. This apparatus was invented in 1715.

Capt. James Bushell seems to have begun his diving work about the year 1700, at which time a large pair of bellows was used - from a boat on the surface - to pump air down to the diver."

The other interesting personage noted by Philip Morant as hailing from Frinton at this time is recorded as follows: "Not far from the Church is a pretty little House and Gardens belonging once to the famous Cornelius a Tilbury, who in King William's reign [i.e. 1650 - 1702], eat a great quantity of poison and yet survived it." Some historians claim that it was Cornelius's house in which Bushell was later to live, but there is no proof of this. In fact, even the existence of Cornelius a Tilbury is so shadowy that the reason for his taking poison and his life after that miraculous recovery cannot now be substantiated.

Having said that all the early parish registers for Frinton are missing we must draw attention to the exception which proves the rule. Copies of entries in the original registers had to be sent to the Bishop of London, in whose diocese Frinton lay. The only copies now existing are those for just two years - 1638 and 1639. So a very few of Frinton's inhabitants do creep into the limelight of recorded history. The complete record for these two years simply shows:

Baptisms 1638 Sep 2 LEE, Simon and Mary, twins of Simon and Mary
1639 None
Marriages 1638 None
1639 Aug 11 MUFFLE Thomas & Elizabeth MOORE
Burials 1638 Nov 4 LEE Simon son of Simon & Mary
Feb 21 LEE, Simon, Parson of this parish
1639 Jul 18 CUTTING, Adery   Signed: Henry Grimston, Rector
                                 Thos. Porter, Churchwarden

In this scrap of record there can be found two useful pieces of information. One is that the population of Frinton at this time was so small that there was only one baptism and one marriage throughout the two years. We know from later maps that even two hundred years on there were no more than five houses and three or four cottages in the whole parish. The other point shown is that while Simon was shown as the parson he was actually the curate installed to do all the work of the parish for the Rector Henry Grimston who was the Lord of the Manor himself or related to him and who lived at the Hall in appropriate style. Simon Lee's death is shown as on or before 21st February, 1638, but we must remember that in those days the New Year began on 'Lady Day', the day of the Annunciation of the Virgin, 25th March, so Simon died, sadly, the February following the birth of the son named after him in the previous September and then his death two months later.

Grimston's Hall has long since gone. We have it on the authority of P and C White: "There have been 2 Manor houses or Halls. The earlier Hall was reported by a 17th Century visitor to be half a mile Northeast of the Church ... we found on the Tithe Map ... drawn up in 1839, a field called "Old Hall Yard".

The site of this field would now be on the foreshore approximately opposite The Crescent and we could reasonably assume that the Old Hall lay to seaward of it, perhaps not quite at the exact half-mile distance nor in the direction noted by our visitor..." Before the sea lapped at the door of the ancient Hall a good deal of the old Frinton fields had been brought down as the soft cliffs yielded to the fiercer storms and higher tides. Before Station Road, now Connaught Avenue, was laid out the 'tree-lined village lane' followed the line of Old Road to the Old Hall. Now it ends in just a footpath across the Greensward and so down the steps to the beach. Once, that lane led beyond the Hall to the real old hamlet of Frinton. Now the parish, practically halved in size can only claim its tiny church as an original building of the ancient settlement, and with its area reduced to some 400 acres it is but a quarter of the size of its inland neighbours and ranks as one of the smallest parishes in the county.

And so we leave Frinton in the seventeenth century, assailed, besieged invested by the forces of nature but seemingly serene in its ignorance of the doings of men and the making of history in the country or the county. Shakespeare's plays saw no performance here, Queen Elizabeth passed it by in her 'Progresses', neither Van den Keere or John Speed deemed Frinton's position worth pin-pointing in their maps of 1605 and 1610. But some gossip must have been muttered round the hamlet when the so-called 'witches' were taken from their homes in the Tendring Hundred in 1649 to be cruelly hanged after 'trial' at the Chelmsford assizes. One of these poor souls came from nearby Thorpe and the Vicar of Clacton witnessed against her. Yet what went on in Chelmsford in those days was as unrelated to Frinton's daily life as what went on in the moon.

As to the Black Art itself, David Coller, one-time Editor of the *Essex Chronicle* and author, in 1841, of *The People's History of Essex*, says, "It was not till the reign of George II that witchcraft ceased to be recognised by the law as a crime. In the 9th year of that monarch an act was passed enacting that no prosecution should be instituted against any person for witchcraft, sorcery, or enchantment. The belief in witches still lingers faintly in some of the rural cottages of the county. The whole brood of imps, however, has vanished before the daylight of advancing education. They no longer walk the earth in visible shapes within the reach of the press or the sight of the village school. The witches who now work their potent spells are not the ugly and wrinkled and ignorant, but those of the bright eye, and peachy cheek, and polished mind; and the only flame to which we consign them is the flame of love."

All that worthy author could find to say on Frinton at this time was that it: "...has been reduced to its present diminutive state by the encroachment of the waves. Its village disappeared beneath their attacks two centuries ago; of its church upon the cliffs a storm in 1703 left only a wreck of the west end, with accommodation for about a dozen worshippers; and the site of the Hall is now some half a mile out at sea. - Robert Hills, Esq., owns part of the lands."

CHAPTER 3

So we come to the eighteenth century and almost immediately meet with disaster. The terrible storm of the night of 26th November, 1703, is probably the worst ever known on the eastern seaboard, approached in intensity only by that of 13th October, 1822. When I tell you that twelve men-of-war, crewed by some 1,800 sailors were blown from their moorings off the Thames estuary, and not a man was saved, you can judge the fury of that gale. This was the night that the famous Essex designer and builder of the first Eddystone lighthouse, Henry Winstanley, was washed to his death from that rock, and all his men with him and not a vestige of his lighthouse remained next day.

Frinton's great loss in the storm was the chancel of its church. It was blown into a total ruin. The community was so small that the rebuilding could not be put in hand at once. There was no such thing as insurance against storm damage at that time and with the Rector an absentee, holding another living, and the Hall leased out by the Lord of the Manor there was no-one of sufficient standing or wealth to undertake or instigate even the essential repairs. The other point was that since there were hardly more than half a dozen worshippers at any one time they and the parson could all be quite comfortably accommodated in the nave.

So it was that, down to enlargement in 1880, Frinton church was visited by the curious sightseer as being the smallest church in England at 22 feet long and 18½ feet wide. Whilst it made the church a tourist attraction it was not strictly true. Lullington church, in Sussex is only 16½ feet long and 16 feet wide, being the surviving chancel of a much bigger thirteenth century church. Since the storm had left the nave open to the weather the quickest, cheapest repair was made - it was simply boarded up.

One of the earliest documents of the eighteenth century still surviving is the lease by Joseph Avery of Kirby-le-Soken (Parson of that place and of Frinton, too) to David Darme, yeoman, of Greensted, near Colchester of the 'parsonage house at Frinton' and its land. The timber on that land was reserved to Avery as was the right to access over the land to get at the timber. He was quite specific in detailing how he wanted the place looked after. The new tenant had to set in hand 40 rods [220 yards] of hedging and ditching, to keep the window glass in good repair and the barns properly and regularly thatched. Only one half of the land was to be ploughed and every year one third of the cultivated land had to be left fallow. The tenant had to pay all taxes on the property except the land tax. When William Martin took up the lease in November, 1716, it was stipulated that at the end of the lease he would leave 8 acres next to the 'four way leet' well- sown with clover seed at no less than 12lbs per acre.

According to the 'List of Rectors', Joseph Avery was instituted as Rector in 1691. From a note in the registers made by the later Churchwarden, Richard

Stone we read: "N.B. The above Jos. Avery was presented by Robt. Warren in 1691 to the Rectory of Frinton which he appears to [have] held until his death in 1719 - but the registers are wanting during Mr. Avery's incumbency thro. Mr Warren's and son's time buried here 1721-22 there is no burial record of them nor of Captain James Bushell drowned 1735 mard. to Joan their sister." Further notes in the burial register by this dedicated churchwarden, give us one or two names of residents in the early days of the eighteenth century:

"James Hinsum of Frinton Wick came to live there at Michaelmas 1738. Ann, wife of the above, died 1756 aged 47 years, buried at the Hythe Church, Colchester. Ann, their eldest daughter, died 1761 and buried at Kirby. Called Ann Hincham in the Kirby register. James, eldest son of James and Ann Hinsum died August, 1766, buried at the Hythe. Mr Hinsum married Debrah Ponder in 1762 and died in 1766 and in 1767 Mrs Hinsum was married at this psh. ch. of Frinton to Sam Strand of Aldham in Suffolk. Mrs Strand died there in 1808 aged 71 years. Her son Saml. Strand told me all his mother cd. remember of Frinton Wick when it was a Brick House and bad dairy land." Since the burial register itself just one burial from 1783 to 1798 inclusive, this account of one Frinton family in detail is all the more important. We will deal with the amazing Mr Stone at length in his own period.

Another family is recalled by Richard Stone and written in the registers in April 1879: "Joseph Swallow of Frinton Hall widower & Elizth. Ram widow married March 31st 1759. The above Mr. Joseph Swallow died in August 1761 - aged 50 years. Elizabeth his wife died at her Father's house - Wm. Flack, Gentln. of Chattisham near Washbrook, Suffolk, the 4th day of June, 1762, aged 40 or 41 years."

Deficient as these registers are in the entry of baptisms, marriages and burials as they happened through the eighteenth century, yet we benefit from these entries made by the churchwarden a hundred years later. The longest account in all the registers is "A receipt or cure for the bite of a mad dog, September 29th 1766"

"a small handful of box
a handful of staggerwort
four red roots of primroses
½ a leaf of bears foot
6d powder of white jasper
5 thimble fulls of julap
4 thimble fulls the powder of steel

Boile the herbs in a pint of new milk 10 minutes, Let it stand till blood warm then mix the powders.

This quantity is to be taken three several morning - shake the bottle & take it fasting & neither eat nor drink for the space of 3 Hours." Could such an amazing concoction be effective? Richard Stone thought so; for he added: "A man took the above who had been bitten and exhibited unequivocal symptoms of hydrophobia. He was tied hand and foot, trying to bite everybody. He was drenched with the medicine "by force". He gradually recovered and lived 30 years afterwards.

The other case was that of Mary Garrett - she took the medicine with great difficulty, but eventually came to live & have a large family. Ricd. Stone - From the *British Medical Journal*."

Rumour about rabies must have been rife around the hamlet at this time, but there was another subject, not recorded in the registers which set the tongues a-wagging from the beginning of the century - and that was smuggling.

The open shore beneath the low cliffs was a really good place for running contraband ashore and Frinton Gap was a reasonable gradient for packhorses to climb to the clifftop and head through the lanes of a practically deserted night-time landscape to hit the high road to London or the Midlands before dawn broke. Smugglers' cutters found a relatively sheltered roadstead off Frinton where they could await the signal from the shore that it was safe to land. In 1721 three finds of smugglers' stores of contraband were discovered. In April, 27 gallons of illicit liquor in casks were found when the revenue men prodded the sands with spiked staves after a tip-off; in July, wagon tracks across the sand above the tide gave the game away and in September, when Doyley, the riding officer, or customs patrolman, was on his usual round his horse stumbled as the ground fell in beneath it to lay open a hoard of 19 ten-gallon casks of brandy.

In 1750 there was a proper fight between the Customs men and the smugglers on the beach between Frinton and Walton. The smugglers set half a dozen vicious dogs on to the officers, then beat them with whips and clubbed them with their own pistols after forcing them to surrender. They threatened them with death if they left their watchhouse that night - and around two o'clock in the morning the inhabitants of Ramsey heard the gang going through with a valuable haul of contraband on pack horses.

Not that these smugglers were likely to come from Frinton, or to involve Frinton people in their get-rich-quick schemes, because the place was still so small that they all knew each other's business. Informers got paid, and smugglers faced a ghastly life in prison. An ecclesiastical return of 1650 states that only four families then lived in Frinton and the parish came very close to being united with Walton and served by the one priest. Fortunately, the idea did not catch on. In 1670 the Hearth Tax returns, listing every house that possessed a hearth, and thus a fire, showed four such houses and the similar return of 1723 showed only one more house. Even as late as 1860 the population was reported as 20 people of all ages living in four 'houses' and four 'cottages'. The poorer families of the four recorded eked out a pretty basic living by their work on the land for the tenant of the Manor and its farm and other landowners around the hamlet.

Mothers and children and perhaps those too old for the hard physical work on the land found a diminutive source of income from collecting copperas on the beach. To explain what that is let me quote from my recently published history of Essex:

"An unusual but important Essex industry closely connected with cloth was the making of a black dye from copperas... Black ink was made from the same stuff. The Portuguese demanded black cloth for their women's conventional wear, so Essex cloth workers who had very valuable export contracts with Portugal, had urgent need of that dye. Copperas occurs naturally on the northeast coast of Essex as twig-like nodules of bisulphate of iron. It was gathered from the beaches by women and children picking it laboriously from the foot of the cliffs where it had been washed out by tidal action. By mixing loads of copperas with layers of scrap iron and damping it all down, the deadly green vitriol, basis of the black dye, and sulphuric acid were produced. It was done on the very foreshore in hazardous conditions. At Walton-on-the-Naze the ground on which this was done became so polluted with sulphur that absolutely nothing grew there for over a hundred years after the practice was discontinued." The Walton copperas house, the largest on the Essex coast was flourishing at this time but then waned with the gradual decline of the local tanning and cloth industries, though the collection of copperas from the beach went on for perhaps another fifty years.

Frinton can claim a particularly interesting reminder of those days. A letter from Thomas Bird of Romford to the *Essex Review* in 1893 reads, " ... I have a brass token in my possession some-what similar to that of the Walton one [dated 1736], and which was probably used for the same purpose, viz., for the payment to the persons collecting copperas, of which there were large quantities on the beach at Frinton as well as at Walton. I recollect both places more than fifty years since, and can testify to the abundance of the one upon the shores at that time. The token is an inch in diameter, and has on the obverse JOHN RICE, in two lines, and on the reverse MANOR OF FRINTON, in three lines."

John Rice had leased the right to gather copperas from the Lord of the Manor as is shown in a deed of 1746 outlining the partition of the various estates of Sir Richard Hopkins, deceased, possessed of, among other lands, "... all the Manor and Lordship ... of Frinton, otherwise Frinton Hall ... Essex with the Rights thereof ... and Right of ... Presentation to the Parish Church of Frinton... And of all that Messuage or Farm House and all those Lands ... in Frinton Kirby and Walton ... now or late in the Tenure or Occupation of William Baker his Assigns or Undertenants at the yearly rent of One Hundred and Fifty-seven Pounds. And also of a liberty of gathering and taking Copperas Stone from the Sea Shore belonging to the said Manor Granted to and now or late ... enjoyed by one John Rice at the yearly rent of Fifteen Pounds ... which by ... Lease and Release bearing Date, twenty fourth Day of June 1731 ... were conveyed to ... Sir Richard Hopkins ... 17th June 1742."

His heirs agreed that lots should be drawn for his property in southern England assembled into two separate groups. Lot A included Frinton for which William Baker was paying a rent of £157 a year and John Rice had to find £15 annually for the 'Copperas Fishing'. Sir Edward Bellamy was lucky enough to draw this Lot. He is shown as the owner and, incidentally, as an Alderman of the City of London, in 1748, when he agreed with the Lords of the Manors of Great and Little Holland as to where their boundaries met on the beach.

Documents of sale, lease and marriage settlement between 1676 and 1730 show how the house and land called 'Crispes' was sold by Lionel Bacon of Coddenham, Suffolk, to Joseph Thurston, a woollen draper of Colchester. In 1676, it came into the possession of Gabriel Shaw and his wife Elizabeth of Kirby and was settled on their only daughter Elizabeth upon her marriage to John King, on 20th January 1730, being leased at the same time to Robert Price of Colchester. At this time Jeremy Watson was Lord of the Manor and exercising his right in the appointment of the Rector. He was followed by Sir Edward Bellamy as we have shown, who was then quickly followed by George Lynn, who we know was presenting the Rector to this living from 1750 to 1757 at least.

The next stage in our story must be the first written and successfully published account of the history of Frinton. It appeared in 1768 as a very small part of The Reverend Philip Morant's huge two volume work, first produced in parts, entitled *The History and Antiquities of Essex*. Frinton occupies just one of the 1165 pages of the 1816 edition. Naturally this great work has been used in the compilation of this specific history of Frinton so it will not be repeated, but some quotations do extend our knowledge of this place in the eighteenth century:

"Sir Ralph Chamberlain was the next possessor of this estate [hence the naming of today's Chamberlain Road]. His granddaughter, Mary Gray, was married to Francis, or Henry Cockain; and, being his widow, in the year 1576, she presented to this living. Their daughter and heir, Dorothy, took for her husband Wm. Pirton, of Little Bentley, Esq., who, in her right, presented to this living in 1586. Of them, this estate was purchased by Edward Grimston, [another modern street name] of Bradfield, Esq. He held his first court here 11th of Aug. 1603; and at the time of his decease, the 16th of Aug. 1610, held the manor of Skirmans-fee alias Frinton-hall, in Frinton and Kirkeby. Sir Harbottle, his son and heir, was created Baronet the 25th of November 1612; and departing this life in 1648, was succeeded by his son, Sir Harbottle Grimston, Bart. His heirs sold this estate to Thomas Warren, of Wapping, mariner, who presented to the rectory in 1691. He married Elizabeth, daughter of John Culmer, of Deal; and had by her, Jeremy, Thomas, Joane, wife of James Bushell of Little Holland, mariner and Martha. Jeremy Warren, the eldest son and heir had, by Elisabeth his wife, daughter of ... Greenglasse, of Suffolk, Gent. two daughters, Lucy and Joanna. Sir Richard Hopkins, Knight, purchased it, and from him it descended to his heir at law, Sir Edw. Bellamy, one of whose daughters brought it to George Lynne, of Southwic, Esq. Frinton Wic[k] belongs to Mr Michael Hills. Thomas Scipper hath also some land in this parish."

James Bushell gets another mention by the unknown jotter of notes in a pocket book concerning the very high tide of 16th February 1736: "Capn. James Bushell - was drowned in the Great Tide - Famous as Fishing for Wrecks - buried near The Church Porch at Frinton." That tide driven by a fierce northwest wind piled itself up on Frinton's cliffs and brought the old church that much closer to the rapacious breakers.

From 1754 we have original documents, kept in Frinton, concerned with Frinton and with the people of the time. That is the date from which the Frinton registers begin. That is to say baptisms from 1754 to 1775 and from 1781 to 1783, and burials from 1762 to 1777 are entered on a bundle of loose sheets with the endorsement, 'registered into proper book'. Alas, that 'proper' register bound in leather, is lost. Marriages entered in a separate book run from 1762 to 1812. From 1813 all parishes had to use new, printed books for each of the three categories of baptisms, marriages and burials, and happily they still exist.

Though this parish was so small in population it still had to have the necessary officers to run its affairs, keeping the peace, looking after the poor and the sick and reporting regularly to church and civil authorities. So there is still in existence the Parish Overseers' Account Book, running from 1776 to 1794. It is headed on the first page, with something of a flourish, "Richard Stone, Overseer and Church warden". Then it informs the reader that the old parish book of Frinton which would have gone back to the days of Good Queen Bess was lost - though a few accounts of the rates collected and paid out from 1738 to 1754 were preserved. Then some officers of the parish are named; Mr. Baker was the Overseer, James Hinsum was a churchwarden and Joseph Swallow is shown as holding one of those posts from 1753 to 1761. Then we have "An account of What Money is disbursed in the Parish of Frinton from Monday, April 8th, 1776, to Monday, March 31st, 1797. These accounts show in some detail who were the poor people in receipt of maintenance from the rates on the property of their richer brethren. They also show the expenses incurred in the day-to-day running of this little outpost of local government.

The Constable is a key figure in these accounts. He was chosen annually. There is an entry in the accounts for 7th July, 1776: "Paid the Constable for a journey to Thorpe to be sworn on to the office - 3s. 6d." This would probably have been for the hire of a horse - still echoed in the 'car allowance' expenses claimed today by local government officers. There are so many entries of money paid out in poor relief that we can only be selective in our examples:

"1776 July 14th Paid for the maintenance of John Beckett's child
14 week att 1s.6. per wk.   £1.1s.0d.

20th Pd. for a pr. of breeches & pr. of Shoes for Guirton Balls
6s.0d.
Oct. 1 To a journey to Thorp to have Walter Snell examined
2s.6d.

This last entry shows how careful the small parish had to be when a person came from elsewhere to settle in Frinton, for if he or she became ill or poverty-stricken they would be another drain on the limited financial resources raised from the poor rate. Such a person was taken before a magistrate and examined closely as to their origin; then, if they became ill or indigent they would be 'passed' from parish to parish, from constable to constable until their official place of settlement was reached.

Reading further we see more of Frinton's inhabitants at this time. For example, Mr. Knock was 'keeping the girl Beckett', Robert Freeman and Ebenezer Jonson, down on their luck, both have five-shilling hand-outs. Freeman, though, is the subject of a sad entry on the following 2nd May: "Paid for a coffin for Rt. Freeman £0.9s.0d. Beside the payment of his nurses in his final hours, and for the beer drunk at his funeral there is also the entry "Paid at Mr Hewitt's Shop 7s.1d. This must be the earliest known record of a shop at Frinton.

As we go through 1779 Richard Stone continues as Churchwarden and Over-seer, and John English becomes Constable. William Tuke was being helped with his rent, Ebenezer was given a chaldron of coals, while widows Freeman and Newman, Beckett's child and 'Boy Balls' were constantly in receipt of financial help. Another unfortunate parishioner comes into the record with the entry "Paid Dr Annis's Bill for Moses Nise leg." The same Moses was being 'kept' by some un-named person on a weekly allowance of five shillings. The whole sum produced by the rate was £21.13s.6d., but in that year the Overseer had disbursed £23.1s.2½d., so he was owed £1.7s.8½d. - to be raised from next year's rate!

The increase in population is shown by more surnames turning up in these records. So far nine families have been identified. Then we find that Richard Box was keeping Moses Nice, Mr Resker made a coat for the Boy English and John Fitch was keeping the boy Freeman. By 1782 fourteen surnames have been mentioned and some division between rich and poor can be seen in entries like:
"1781 Sep 30 Paid Robert Cooper for the widow Newman's House rent and fireing for one year £2.10s.0d.

On the same day Richard Box was paid an annual fee of 10s.6d. for being Church Clerk. On 2nd April, 1782, the same man was appointed Constable and then served as an overseer from 1784. That was the year when poor old Moses Nice died and sixteen shillings was paid out for his coffin. His shroud of baize cost 4s.0d. and Robert Harris was allowed £1.11s.6d. for the bedding he had provided for Moses' last days. The last entry in the book - after April, 1794 - is a receipt signed by the physician Samuel Newton:

"1793 Aug 5 - Mr Burrell of Frinton paid me Two Guineas for attending ye paupers in past."

Now let us look at that other fount of knowledge of Frinton - the Parish registers. We are in luck here because, although there are very few entries indeed of baptisms, marriages and burials, the conscientious churchwarden, Richard Stone, living in the next century has filled the blank pages with all kinds of local information. Even before the Baptisms begin in April, 1738. Mr Stone has filled a page with "An account of the Great Tide, 1874", the death of a vicar, complete with rhyming epitaph, and accounts of the weather for various years between 1779 and 1880. They will all be dealt with in their due places in this history.

The earliest baptism recorded is that of James, the son of James and Anne Hinsum, who was born on February 13th and baptised on 16th April, 1738. Then follow these entries:

"James, son of Robert and Sarah Freeman was born ye 18th Sep & Baptiz'd ye 1st of Octo. 1738.

John son of James & Anna Hinsum was born ye 6 Nov & Baptiz'd ye 10th of Decembr. 1741.

Samuel son of Robert & Sarah Freeman was born Sep 5th & Baptiz'd ye 28 of Sepbr. 1740."

Four more children of these parents were born and baptized between 1742 and 1750. Two new names crop up in 1752, when Daniel, son of John and Anna Daniels, was born and in 1756 when Mary, daughter of John and Sarah English, was baptised.

Then follows a note that for seven years no record was kept of the baptisms performed. Frinton was served by a poorly paid curate because the Rector was a pluralist - he held one or more other livings and, by putting in curates to do the work for very low pay led a grand life. The curates had very little interest in the parish and often did not bother to keep the records in good order. This is proved by the memorandum written in 1872 by Richard Stone, the voluble churchwarden: "The Revd. Richd. Willan, M.A., Curate of Frinton from the year 1800 till 1817 was Vicar of Gt. Clacton, Essex from 1769 till 1822 being the space of 53 years."

Burials are rarely recorded; one only is shown between 1783 and 1787, and only one more down to 1798. Richard Stone, son of the Richard Stone, church-warden at this time, records on 28th May, 1876: "The Revd. Foak [sic, i.e. Frank] Beadle, the newly inducted rector took from Richard Stone the marriage register from 1762 and the Births, Marrs. & Deaths registers 1813 - 1875"... to have them in his custody as they had always been in mine and my family ... The very oldest register book for Frinton down to the years 1760, 1761 irrevocably lost."

We shall end the story of Frinton's progress, or lack of it, through this century with the comment of an unknown author who compiled a collection of architectural notes on churches in Essex between 1790 and 1799:

"July 18th, 1790. Frinton com. [county of] Essex.

A neat but very small church, the parish containing but four houses, except a few cottages. It has been much larger as appears by the ruins at the East end, but being greatly decayed was partly pulled down, & made less about A.D. 1743. In the East windows are ... arms in old Stained Glass."

INSTRUCTIONS
For Constables.

At a Petty Sessions, held the 23rd day of February, 1829, at the Maid's Head Inn, situate in Thorpe, in the Hundred of Tendring, in the County of Essex,

WE the undersigned, being Justices of our Sovereign Lord the King, assigned to keep the Peace in and for the said County, DO recommend that in each Parish within this Division, means should be used to impress the Constables with the nature and importance of their Office, and to direct their attention to a diligent discharge of their several and important Duties, particularly in making proper Presentments to the Magistrates, and in enforcing due Order and Regulation in the Public Houses within their respective Districts and Parishes.——The Justices aforesaid, therefore think it incumbent upon them to give the Constables the following Instructions, and at the same time to remind them, that the Laws have provided Punishment for their Neglect of Duty.

J. MARTIN LEAKE.

| R. W. COX. | THOMAS NUNN. |
| H. R. SOMERS SMITH. | THOMAS NUNN, JUN. |

To Mr. _Richard Ann_ ———— Constable of the Parish of _Frinton_ – – – in the County of Essex.

IT is your duty, as Constable, to visit Alehouses frequently, at times when you are not expected, and to see that no irregularities are permitted.

To prevent Drunkenness by giving notice to the Magistrates of such as are guilty of it.

To prevent Gaming, and to give notice to Justices of those who keep Houses in which Gaming of any kind is permitted. To seize E.O. Tables, or any other Tables or Implements of Gaming, used at Fairs or other Public Meetings.

To prevent abuses of the Lord's-day commonly called Sunday, such as Tippling in Alehouses during Divine Service, using Dogs, Guns, Snares, Nets, or other Engines for Killing or Destroying Game, and using Games or Pastimes, following Worldly Callings, or Travelling with Waggons, Wains, or other Carriages, or Driving Cattle.

To carry before a Magistrate such Persons as are guilty of Profane Swearing and Cursing, if they are unknown to you, or to give notice to Magistrates, if they are known to you.

To apprehend and carry before a Magistrate, every Person being able wholly or in part to maintain himself, or herself, or family, by work or other means, and wilfully refusing or neglecting so to do, by which he or she, or his or her family, shall have become chargeable to the Parish.

To apprehend and carry before a Magistrate every Person returning to and becoming chargeable to the Parish from whence he or she shall have been legally removed, without a Certificate from the Churchwardens or Overseers of the Poor of some other Parish, acknowledging him or her to be settled there.

To apprehend and carry before a Magistrate every Petty Chapman or Pedlar, wandering abroad and trading without being duly Licensed.

To apprehend and carry before a Magistrate every Prostitute wandering about in the Public Streets, or Public Highways, or in any place of public resort, and behaving in a riotous or indecent manner.

To apprehend and carry before a Magistrate every Person wandering abroad, or placing himself or herself in any Public Place, Street, or Highway, Court, or Passage, to Beg or gather Alms, or causing or procuring, or encouraging any Child or Children so to do.

To apprehend and carry before a Magistrate every Person wandering abroad and Lodging in any Barn or Out-House, or in any Deserted or Unoccupied Building.

To apprehend and carry before a Magistrate every Person exposing to view in any Street, Road, Highway, or Public Place, any Obscene Print, Picture, or other Indecent Exhibition.

To apprehend and carry before a Magistrate every Person wandering abroad and endeavouring by the exposure of Wounds or Deformities to obtain or gather Alms, or endeavouring to procure Charitable Contributions of any kind under false pretences.

To apprehend and carry before a Magistrate every Person running away and leaving his Wife and Family Chargeable to the Parish.

To apprehend and carry before a Magistrate every Person Playing or Betting in any Street, Road, Highway, or other Open and Public Place, at or with any Table or Instrument of Gaming, at any Game, or pretended Game of Chance.

To apprehend and carry before a Magistrate any Person found in or upon any Dwelling House, Warehouse, Coach-house, Stable, or Out-house, or any enclosed Yard, Garden, or Area, for unlawful purposes.

To apprehend and carry before a Magistrate every Person who shall wilfully or maliciously do or commit any Damage, Injury, or Spoil, to or upon any Building, Wall, Fence, Hedge, Gate, Stile, Guide Post, Milk Stone, Tree-wood, Under-wood, Orchard, Garden, Nursery, Ground Crops, Vegetables, Plants, Land, or other matter or thing growing or being thereon; to or upon any real or personal property of any nature or kind whatsoever.

To prevent Nuisances of every description, by giving notice of those who commit them.

To prevent Affrays and Breaches of the Peace, by requiring the Offenders to depart peaceably, and by apprehending them if they refuse so to do.

To give notice to the nearest Magistrate whenever you hear of any Unlawful Assembly, Mob, or Concourse of People.

To prevent Persons from throwing Fire Works, Squibs, Rockets, &c. &c. in the Public Streets or Highways, by apprehending them if they will not desist.

To attend in case of any Fire breaking out by Night or by Day, and to assist in putting it out, and preventing Persons from Plundering.

To give notice to the Magistrates of Persons who are guilty of Selling Unwholesome Provisions of any kind.

To give notice of Persons using False Weights or Measures, or Bakers, Chandlers, or other Dealers who sell their Articles contrary to the Assize.

To apprehend and carry before a Magistrate Persons having in their possession Bundles of Wood, Poles, Rails, Posts, &c. suspected to have been stolen.

To apprehend and carry before a Magistrate Persons reasonably suspected of being Deserters from his Majesty's Service.

To apprehend and carry before a Magistrate Persons charged with Felony, and if necessary to command the assistance of by-standers, to confine Felons or put them in Irons if necessary, to prevent an escape when you are taking them before a Magistrate, or to Gaol.

To raise a hue and cry for pursuing and apprehending an Offender when a Felony is committed, and he flies for the same.

To provide Carriage on the Marching of Soldiers.

To execute Warrants without delay, to bring the Offenders before the Magistrate who granted them (if specially mentioned) or otherwise, before the nearest Magistrate, to hold the Offenders in Custody till discharged by the Magistrate, or till they are delivered into the custody of the Gaoler, and in serving a Summons to make the contents known to the party to whom it is granted, and to attend at the Time and Place set forth in the Summons, to acquaint the Magistrate with what you have done.

And the following Articles of Inquiry are to be answered by you upon Oath, whenever you are called upon so to do by the Magistrates at their Petty or Special Sessions.

ALEHOUSES.—Are there any Persons in your Parish, who sell Ale or Spirituous Liquors without a License?

How often, and on what days have you visited the Alehouses since your last return?

Did you visit them at uncertain times when the Publicans had no notice of your coming?

Did you find them free from Tippling, Gaming, and other disorders?

Have you regularly visited them on Sundays before the commencement of Divine Service? and did you know that you visited them had them cleared from Company?

Do the Persons who keep Alehouses sell their Liquor in Mugs or other Vessels of full measure?

Are their Houses shut up at night at Ten o'clock?

DRUNKENNESS. — Have you given notice to the Magistrates of those who are guilty of Drunkenness or Tippling?

GAMING.—Do you know of any Houses in your Parish in which Gambling of any description is committed?

Have you been careful to prevent Gambling at Fairs or other Public Meetings within your Parish?

LORDS-DAY, OR SUNDAY.—Have you given notice to the Magistrates of those who amuse themselves with Idle Sports on Sunday?

Of those who exercise their worldly calling on that day?

Of Carriers or others travelling with Horses, Wains, or other Carriages?

Of Drovers travelling with Cattle?

INDECENT PUBLICATIONS.—Have you given notice to the Magistrates of Persons publicly selling, or suspected of secretly selling, indecent and improper Publications?

Have you apprehended any Persons singing indecent and seditious songs?

VAGRANTS.—Have you apprehended any Persons whom you found begging, Petty Chapmen wandering abroad without a License, Persons of evil fame, Prostitutes, Reputed Thieves, and such as had Instruments of House breaking upon them?

ASSAULTS, &c.—Have you been careful to prevent Breaches of the Peace, by apprehending the Offenders when they refused to depart peaceably?

NUISANCES.—Do you know of any Nuisances such as carrying Offensive Materials into the Highways, laying Obstructions in the Highways, stopping up Watercourses, leaving dangerous holes, Pits, Pounds, or Ditches uncovered by Rails, suffering Ruinous Buildings to remain, which are in danger of falling upon His Majesty's Subjects, suffering Hogs to run at large in the Street, or any other nuisance.

N.B. You are enjoined to attend to the foregoing Instructions, and to bring them with you when you make your return to the Petty or Special Sessions.

The following is a Table of Fees, recommended to be paid to the Constables by the Magistrates for the Execution of their Duty.

	£.	s.	d.
For the Oath of Office	0	1	0
For the Service of any Warrant or Summons in the Parish	0	1	0
For every Mile beyond the limits of the Parish, per Mile	0	0	6
If the distance of Ten Miles	0	5	0
For every Journey exceeding Ten Miles, and when the Constable is absent the whole day, (including expenses)	0	10	0
For attending the Magistrates at their Petty Sessions in addition to the Mileage	0	1	0
Attending the Coroner with notice of a death according to the above calculation of Time and Mileage			
For summoning the Jury and attending the Inquisition	0	10	0
For expense of Jury			
Verifying a List of Jurors to return to the Quarter Session	0	1	0

HADDON, PRINTER, MARKET PLACE, MANNINGTREE.

CHAPTER 4

The nineteenth century opened so peacefully in Frinton, but unbeknown to ordinary folk there was a plan afoot that would make a big impact on the local scene. It all came about because Napoleon Bonaparte led his country to one success after another in conquering countries and adding to empire. In 1793 France declared war on England, seriously threatening an invasion. Great alarm brought rapid government action. Signal towers where men could ceaselessly watch the North Sea were built on selected sites from St Osyth to Harwich and completed by the spring of 1795. The one most important to our story was erected on the cliffs at the northernmost end of the parish, roughly at the end of Pole Barn Lane. It is specially marked on the Ordnance Survey map of 1805. It was flanked by two other signal towers at Little Holland and Great Clacton.

In the same year the Board of Ordnance, responsible for the defence of our shores, declared in favour of building gun batteries round the coast where an invasion might be expected. By 1797 such batteries were established on the Essex coast - one of them on the very southernmost edge of the parish of Frinton. It is mentioned in the *Ipswich Journal* of 14th June, 1800:

"The guns at Frinton Battery, on the Essex coast, were fired on the King's Birthday at noon, in honour of the same, and Mr Stone of that place had a party of friends who in the afternoon met Lieut. Stokes and the Sea Fencibles at the Battery where many loyal songs, accompanied with instrumental music, were sung, and the spectators were regaled with plenty of good old beer till sunset, when the party returned to Mr Stone's house, and spent the remainder of the evening with great conviviality." That Battery was also honoured with a visit by the Duke of York, as Field Marshal, on 28th September, 1801. The *Essex Journal* tells us he "inspected troops of Colchester barracks at Lexden Heath, then the following morning with Marquess Cornwallis, Gen. Dundas and other Staff Officers went on to Frinton and inspected its battery ..."

That Battery is shown clearly on the Tithe Map of 1839, and as late as 1861 the cottage built on the site was still called Frinton Battery. Even today older inhabitants refer to it as Battery Point, though the Golf Club has replaced it in terms of giving directions to visitors. Unknown to most of the local people, Sir John Moore (1761-1809), the famous general, came to Frinton with Major Hay of the Royal Engineers in October, 1797, had a good look at the beach and the cliffs to the left and right of it and declared: "... the line favourable for landing is therefore supposed to lie between Walton Gap and Clacton Wick, a distance of eight miles." That was the reason for siting the battery at Frinton. The carting of the stone and the bricks, the sand and lime, and, most of all, the guns, must have been a talking point in the hamlet, and a sight to be seen for months.

Then Napoleon reckoned that such an invasion was unlikely to succeed, so, in 1798, he turned his attention to Egypt and India. He was frustrated by Nelson at the Battle of the Nile on 1st August, 1798, and peace was ultimately negotiated in March, 1802. By 16th May of the following year war with France had broken out again and a landing on the Frinton section of coast was still much feared. Accordingly a system of defensive towers was set interlocking with those gun batteries which had still not been tested by the French.

They were called Martello Towers because the pattern originated in Mortella, Corsica, where they had proved a powerful deterrent to attack.

The towers on the Essex coast were built by men of the Royal Engineers. Seven sites were compulsorily purchased, but the haggling involved held up the work until 1810. Each tower needed more than 700,000 bricks to produce a vast bulk weighing some 2,300 tons. In the official files the towers were identified alphabetically. 'T' was for Frinton. It is amusing to read the official report of General Mann in 1812: "All the Towers are supplied with Berths for the Troops & Grates for Cooking. But owing to The Storekeeper's department not having yet procured axles for the drawbridge or Hinges for the Doors, the Towers cannot be reported ready for delivery to the Ordnance Barrack Department." - there were echoes of that state of readiness in 1914 and in 1939!

The 1815 Battle of Waterloo ended any further French threat, so the Frinton tower was never manned. A report by the Board of Ordnance in 1812 stated that "... circumstances necessary to be considered, as the unhealthiness of the Coast, would render it inadvisable to place the troops in the Towers and Batteries till threatened with an attack. Fortunately Weely Barracks are centrally situated to all parts of Clacton Beach and are within two hours march of any of the Towers and Batteries in this Quarter. The Garrison may therefore be placed in these Barracks till summoned to the Beach." Frinton Tower would have housed some fifty men in time of war, but the only man to live in it was a married pensioner of the Royal Engineers, stationed there from 1816 to look after it on a care and maintenance footing, receiving an extra shilling a day on his pension.

Kenneth Walker, to whom I am indebted for this specialist information, sums up the last chapter in the story of this great landmark: "The site of this is the western extremity of Frinton Greensward. The Battery had already been erected when the 6½ acres, part of Great Hanging and Boat Fields, were purchased in January, 1811, from William Lushington of Tunbridge Wells, owner of Frinton Hall ... and other gentlemen. The land was sold in January, 1822, to W L Shadwell. The Tower was presumably pulled down shortly after, though a cottage standing nearby, and known as 'Battery House' was still there in 1876."

Over the same period there was the strange situation that, from the very same stretch of coast guarded by the Towers, Essex seamen sailed on regular trips across to France where French agents were ready to forget hostilities in the interests of smuggling. It was those costly wars with France which added high taxes to just about every item used in daily life and thus made the cheaper prices of smuggled goods a very lucrative trade. It may be that one or two boats pushed off from Frinton beach on a calm sea on a moonless night. They were not necessarily manned by Frinton men.

From the voluminous notes penned by the churchwarden Richard Stone during the last half of the nineteenth century we can even get comments in the parish registers on the local climate like this:

"1797. A gloomy & very wet time for Harvest wh[ich] was late.

"1799. The wettest Harvest on record gloomy & wet & Harvest did not begin till about September 4th - my Father & old Sammy Dennis both told me this... " The next document to help us on our way through the Frinton story is dated 24th June, 1810. It is a 'terrier' or description of the Rectory of Frinton, the lands belonging to it and the people who paid tithes on the land they occupied. It is worth quoting in full:

"First a house Near the Road leading to Kirby consisting of 2 rooms on the Ground Floor 16 feet square each with 2 Rooms over in the Roof, and a small wash house. All Built with Wood Covered with Tiles. A Small Barn & Stables Built with Wood & Thatched, The Glebe 25 Acres X in 6 Fields, adjoining the Hall Land Belonging To Wm Lushington Esqr. & Mrs Mary Gibson.
Also 31 Acres of Land joining Philip Hills Esqr. and the Whole Rented at £32 pr. year.

	£.	s.	d.
Tythe of the Hall Land 200 Acres	60	0	0
Tythe of Philip Hills 120 do.	42	0	0
Do. Mrs. Elizabeth Barnard 19 do.	6	10	0
Tythe Mr. Benjn. Carrington 26 do.	8	0	0
Tythe Mr. Peter Bromley 17½ do	6	0	0
Tythe Mr. Saml. Baker 9 do.			0
Tythe Mr. Thos. Cooper 4 do.		12	0

395½   124   2   0

E G Charnock - Rector

Richard Stone - Churchwarden

Wood belonging to the Glebe Land
Timber Trees very small About 10 X
Pollards Ditto   About 20 z

The Wood was stubbed in 1802 & the Woodfields laid down to grass by order of the Revd. J V Luke, Rector of Frinton, in 1861 by Richd. Stone & his son Wm. Stone."

It can be seen from the last two dates mentioned that Richard added his own comments concerning the Terrier at a later date. He had the rather unpleasant task of being go-between when the Rector fell out with the substantial farmer

James Firman over the matter of payment of tithes which brought about this unusual declaration:

"To Mr. James Firmin

I hereby give you notice that I shall take in kind the Tithes of Corn, Hay, Wood, Lamb, Milk and all other tithable matters and things which shall grow, renew, arise, happen or increase upon or out of the lands and Hereditaments occupied by you in the Lordship or Liberties of Frinton in the county of Essex which will become due to me as the rector of the Parish of Frinton from and after the twenty ninth day of September next, or if that be the Termination of the Composition Year then from and after the day of the present Composition whatever day that may be. And I will not accept any Composition in lieu thereof. And I do hereby require you to set out your Tithes in time accordingly.

Witness my hand this third day of February 1808,
Witness: Bentley Warren   E G Charnock
Febry. 1808 Delivered a true copy hereof to the above named
                                                   Richd. Stone

The Rector was perfectly within his rights to demand this payment in kind because it was not until 1836 that the Tithe Act converted the right to receive a tenth of the produce into an annual rent-charge on the land itself. But I would suggest that in this case the Rector, not satisfied with the level of tithe-rent over previous years was using this ploy to negotiate an increase. By 1818 the Reverend E G Charnock was dead. On 7th November "Frances Vyvyan Loke, A.M. of St. Peters College, Cambridge and Chaplain to the Earl of Wemyss & March was inducted to this living on the death of the Rev. E G Charnock." He was the Rector but he still employed a curate. We are told by the churchwarden that John Kirby, who died in 1830, had been curate for about 30 years. He was succeeded by I J Brusher and then the Revd. W Green, Vicar of Little Clacton took on the curacy of Frinton as well and took his first service on 2nd October, 1859. He continued to Easter 1876 at the princely stipend of £40 which the Bishop eventually increased to £60.

We can thank Churchwarden Stone for further information on that James Firman from whom the Rector claimed his tithes in 1808: "In memory of James Firmin & Eleanor his wife. He departed this life January, 1824 aged 40, leaving a widow & a family of eleven children at Frinton Wick almost unprovided for - she struggled on with her large Family till March 1844, when she was obliged to lease the Farm and afterwards had to live with her daughter Diana at Brentwood where she died from the effects of an accident - aged 70 years. She was the one who had to deal with the assessment for taxes for the year ending 5th April, 1824, but apparently still outstanding on 26th June, 1828. The schedule names but two inhabitants - James Firmin, death not acknowledged, had to pay £4.15s.3d. duty on his 18 windows; £1.7s.6d. on his cart and £1 on his greyhound. Richard Stone had 15 windows in his house and 6 in his cottage - a total of £3.13s.3d. and 8s. on his house dog.

Mrs Firman certainly did try to keep her head above water. In the *Essex Standard* of 29th June, 1833, there appears this advertisement:

"Frinton, near Walton, apartments to let, 2 Sitting Rooms, 3 Bedrooms, Servants' Kitchen, 2 Bedrooms over, commanding a most beautiful view of the sea, distance from Walton 2 miles, and not more than 4 minutes from the Beach. Enquire of Mrs Firman of the same."

Another useful document which has survived to give a glimpse into the state of Frinton in 1821 is the assessment made "... in Pursuance of an Act passed in the 38th year of his Majesty's Reign for granting an aid to his Majesty by a Land Tax to be raised in Great Britain for the Service of the year 1798" - and other later Acts - including "... a Duty on Pensions, Officers and Personal Estates." It shows owners of the land to be William Lushington, Phillip Hills, Elizabeth Barnard, William Micklefield, the Rev. Mr Luke, Mrs Hearn, B Carrington and T D Cooper, Esq. Of the occupiers Richard Stone was a tenant of Lushington, James Firman of Hills, Samuel Baker of Mickelfield and Peter Bromley of Mrs Hearn. The rest occupied their own property, including that T D Cooper who has significance in a later chapter.

Richard Stone, the ever-busy churchwarden, was the Assessor and Collector. He turns up under another hat on 23rd February, 1829, when he is addressed as the Constable of the Parish of Frinton and issued with an exhaustive list of "Instructions for Constables" by the Petty Sessions sitting at the Maid's Head in Thorpe. This shows just how wide-ranging were the poor man's responsibilities - although in this small parish it cannot have been an arduous task. He had another job wished upon him in 1831 when he had to fill out the printed enquiry form giving full details of Frinton's population in the following way:

Inhabited houses	5
Houses building	nil
Houses uninhabited	nil
Families employed in agriculture	6
Employed in Trade, Manufacture, etc	nil
All other families	nil

Males - 12, Females - 23
Males over 20 years - 7
Male servants Upwards of 20 years - 1
      Under 20 years - 1
All female servants - 1   Total - 35

It was the Tithe Act of 1836 which set in hand the first detailed map of the place. No other map since then has given such detail, It was necessary because every piece of property land or water, house and barn had to be clearly shown in

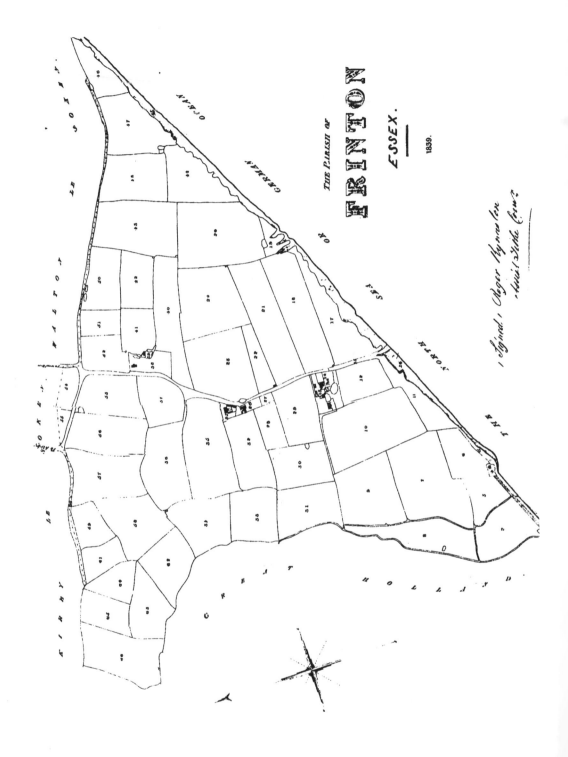

THE PARISH OF

FRINTON

ESSEX.

1839.

Plot	Name	Quality	Size	Landowner	Occupier
1	The Wall	Waste	0.3.37	#	*
2	Old Marsh	P	8.0.24	#	*
3	Boat Field	A	4.0.39	#	*
4	Cottage & garden		0.1.11	¶	§
5	Cliff Piece	Waste	0.2.16	¶	§
6	Tower Ground	A	5.0.33	¶	§
7	Great Hangings	A	15.3.38	#	*
8	Long Marsh	P	9.0.20	#	*
9	Grass Hangings	P	11.3.04	#	*
10	Stackyard Field	A	16.1.10	#	*
11	Smiths Pightle	A	4.1.27	#	*
12	Chapel Field	A	5.0.30	#	*
13	The Hall		3.0.09	#	*
14	Churchyard & church		0.1.34	=	
15	Gapway Drift		0.2.17	#	*
16	The Cliffs		11.0.09	#	*
17	Sea Field	A	8.0.18	#	*
18	Great Cowletts	A	12.0.28	#	*
19	Old Hall Yards	P	1.2.23	#	*
20	Hall Field	A	15.2.32	#	*
21	Pathway Field	A	12.0.18	#	*
22	Cowletts Mead	P	3.0.24	#	*
23	Upper Cowletts	A	12.0.11	#	*
24	Lower Cowletts	A	12.2.32	#	*
25	Homestead		0.3.29	^	+
26	Orchard Piece	P	0.1.34	^	+
27	Garden	A	0.1.20	^	+
28	Pightle		3.1.04	^	+
29	Pump Field	A	7.1.05	^	+
30	Middle Chapel Field	A	7.1.30	^	+
31	Lower Chapel Field	A	8.1.00	^	+
32	Kitchen Field	A	8.0.08	^	+
33	Lower Bull Hill	A	7.2.21	^	+
34	Great Bull Hill	A	8.1.37	^	+
35	Burn Field	A	13.0.04	^	+
36	Hangings	A	10.2.06	^	+
37	Pond Field	A	6.0.14	^	+
38	Parsonage House		0.0.34	=	*
39	Parsonage Mead	P	2.2.14	=	*
40	Long Field	A	9.1.06	=	*
41	Parsonage 4 Acres	A	4.2.10	=	*
42	Partridge Field	A	5.2.36	=	*
43	12 Acre Shreddings	A	12.3.30	#	*
44	First Floody Shots	A	8.0.35	#	*
45	The Cliffs		1.2.05	¬	>
46	Cliff Field	A	4.1.30	¬	>
47	Further Floody Shots	A	9.2.38	#	*
48	9 Acre Shreddings	A	9.1.17	#	*
49	The Lane		0.3.00	#	*
50	Parsonage 6 Acres	A	6.3.04	=	*
51	Parsonage 3 Acres	A	3.1.03	=	*
52	Toll Gate Field	A	5.0.03	=	*
53	Winn Corner	A	7.2.19	^	+
54	Frinton Corner	A	2.1.04	¬	>
55	Whitton Wood	A	0.3.34	¬	>
56	Long 8 Acres	A	9.1.13	^	+
57	White Post Field	A	10.2.05	^	+
58	Wood Field	A	9.3.10	^	+
59	Whitton Wood	W	4.2.05	^	^
60	Whitton Wood Lane		0.2.09	^	+
61	Parsonage Wood Field		3.2.25	=	*
62	Lower 7 Acres	A	7.2.10	^	+
63	Further 6 Acres	A	6.2.39	^	+
64	4 Acres	A	4.0.06	‡	†
65	5 Acres	A	4.3.37	‡	†
66	10 Acres	A	10.2.34	‡	†

A = arable, P = pasture, W = wood

\# = Charlotte Lushington, Edward Homer Reynard, Isaac Stafford Browne

* = Richard Stone, jnr.

= = Revd. Francis Vyvyan Luke

¶ = Hon. Board of Ordnance

§ = William Thompson

^ = Robert Hills

+ = Eleanor Firmin

‡ = Elizabeth Barnard

† = John Dennis Daniels

¬ = Jackson Hunt

> = Samuel Baker

order that the 'Award' of monetary compensation for the cessation of the church's right to tithes could be accurately assessed and shown on the accompanying parchment sheets which are still called the 'Award' in the Essex Record Office where they are carefully preserved. Frinton's map and award were completed in 1839, to operate from 1840, so everyone who wishes can see the definitive record of Frinton at that time - a map on which every field is deliniated and every building from church to farm, from Manor House to cottage, and including the site of a Martello Tower, is marked with a number. On the award that number is repeated, and against it full particulars of the property are given - owner, occupier; if land, whether it is Arable, grass, pasture or wood, and the exact measurement of the area it occupies.

Together the map and the award show that the parish of Frinton was split up between twelve owners - only one of whom lived on his own property - and that was Thomas Cooper who owned and farmed his own three-acre field called Hodge Knowl. Occupiers of the houses and the land number only eight, including Thomas Cooper. The illustration cannot do justice to this amazing map which was drawn to a scale of just over 9 inches to a mile.

The principal owners of land were the Lushington, Reynard and Browne families who had shared in the inheritance of the Lordship of the Manor and its 26 fields. Robert Hills owned some 20 fields and buildings, as well as Whitton Wood. The Reverend Francis Vyvyan Luke is shown as landowner against church and churchyard. He was also the official owner of the Parsonage and its three fields - Parsonage Six Acres, Parsonage Three Acres and Toll Gate Field. The fields, totalling some 15 acres, were farmed by Richard Stone, junior. The last-named field reminds us of the system introduced in the eighteenth century by which private companies undertook to keep parish roads, especially the highways, in good repair by setting up tollgates and charging the travellers directly, thus relieving small parishes like Frinton of an impossible financial burden.

Other absentee landlords from whom fields were rented were Michael Hawes from whom William Tillet rented eleven fields, including the strangely named Botany Bay, just over an acre of grassland. The probable reason for its name is that it was situated so far away from the centre, squeezed in between Thorpe-le-Soken, Great Holland and Little Clacton. Some humorist must have remarked that 'it was just about as far away as Australia'. Elizabeth Barnard did not live in the parish; she let out three-, four-, and-Ten-acre fields to John Dennis Daniels. And if the 1841 Census is to be believed neither he nor Tillet was a local inhabitant. The man who did live locally who farmed no less than 28 fields was Richard Stone, junior.

Proof of the existence of the Martello-tower is found in the listing of three pieces of ground owned by the Honourable Board of Ordnance and occupied by a William Thompson. They are named 'Cottage and Garden', Cliff Piece, and

'Tower Ground'. Widow Eleanor Firmin is shown still trying to make a go of Frinton Wick and its twelve fields adding up to 80 acres or so.

For full details of the all the other people who lived in Frinton we must turn to the national census of 1841. Earlier censuses, every ten years from 1801,had aimed only at providing statistics of national population. The 1841 census included the names of every person in each house on 7th June. No relationship between the individuals living in any one house is shown, that was to come in 1851. Since Frinton was such a small place we can quote that Census in full:

Inhabited houses N[o]	Inhabitants	Age	Occupation	Born in Essex? Y[es] or
1	Richard Stone	31	Farmer	Y
	Mary Ann	33		N
	Richard	5		Y
	Charles	4		Y
	Henry	3		Y
	Mary	2		Y
	Frederick	1 day		Y
	Sarah Rand	47	Ind.[ependent]	N
	Elizabeth Laker	24	Governess	N
	Margaret Gallant	70	Nurse	Y
	Sarah Brett	22	f[emale] s[ervant]	Y
	Eliza Harvey	15	f. s.	Y
	John Dillerson	16	m. s.	Y
1	John Firmin	26	Farmer	Y
	Emma	20		Y
	Harriet	18		Y
	Isabella	17		Y
	Charlotte Parmenter	15	f. s.	Y
	Robert Cross	15	m. s.	Y
1	Samuel Harvey	50	Ag. Lab.	Y
	Sarah	45		Y
	Phebe	16		Y
	Richard	10		Y
	Christian Watts	25		Y
1	William Hayhoe	48	Farmer	Y
1	John Phillips	25	Dissenting Minister	N
1	Thomas Dillerson	56	Ag. Lab.	Y
	Sarah	48		Y
	Elizabeth	14		Y
	William	11		Y
	Ann	7		Y
	Martha	4		Y

1	James Rivers	41	Ag. Lab.	Y
	Susannah	36		Y
	Betsy	12		Y
	Susannah	10		Y
	Ann	8		Y
	John	5		Y
	Sarah	4		Y
	James	2		Y
	William	3		Y
1	Martin Sallows	20	Ag. Lab.	Y
	Hannah	20		Y
	Hannah	3		Y

These then, were the 'happy few' who worked the land on which they lived and went out of the parish for all the shops and the craftsmen to provide them with their daily needs. In their rural isolation and innocence they gave their constable little cause to exercise the full weight of his office. For want of that kind of excitement we end this chapter with a brief history to these times, as set out in William White's *History, Gazetteer and Directory of the County of Essex*, of 1848. This is the earliest entry for Frinton found in a county directory:

"Frinton, a small parish on the sea-coast, 2½ miles S.S.W. of Walton on the Naze, has only 44 inhabitants, 470 acres of land, four houses, and a few cottages, though it is said to have anciently had a village, which was washed away by the ocean at least two centuries ago, and since then the sea has continued to encroach annually upon the land, undermining the cliffs. Pyrites used formerly to be gathered on the beach, for the manufacture of copperas. Miss Charlotte Lushington is the lady of the manor of Frinton, or Skyrman's Fee, and the other principle landowners are Rt. Hills, Esq., E H Reynard, Esq., and the representatives of the late I S Brown. The old Hall was pulled down about 1720, and its site is now in the sea. The present Hall is occupied by a farmer, and the other three houses are the Parsonage (a small cottage occupied by a labourer,) the Wick, and the Battery House ... The rectory ... is in the patronage of E H Reynard, Esq., and the incumbency of the Rev. Fras. Vyvyan Luke, for whom the Rev. J L Kirby, of Little Clacton officiates. The glebe is 28 a(cres), and the tithes were commuted in 1841, for £150 per annum. The FARMERS are, Richard Stone, Hall; Joseph Sadler, Lodge; and Charles Theedam, Wick."

CHAPTER 5

When the time arrived for the Census of Frinton to be taken - on 28th April, 1851, it comes as no surprise to us to find that Richard Stone was the 'Enumerator' - going from door to door to collect the detailed information. He started at his own home, Frinton Hall, where, over the ten years since the last census his wife Mary Ann had presented him with another three children - William, Rosa and Jessie. Elizabeth Laker, now 34 and still single, continued as Governess to the growing family, but the two servants were replaced by the Farrance girls from Kirby-le-Soken; Mary Ann, 20 was Dairy Maid and Lucy, 18, was House Maid. Stone's 'Corn man etc.' and his shepherd were in the Hall at the time and so had to be included. This census gives more information than its predecessor, including the fact that Richard Stone farmed 250 acres, employing 8 men and 3 boys.

From home he set out up the Kirby road to the two cottages where the Snares lived. William, a 78-year-old widower is shown as farming 78 acres, with his 55-year-old son and daughter-in-law next door no doubt helping him out. Back down the other end of the parish, right on the cliff was Battery House, but Richard would not have needed to trek all that way just to enter that it was uninhabited, because he would have known that already, being as he was at the very centre of everything that went on in the parish. Just two more calls and the job would be finished. One was at Frinton Wick, home of another farmer, Charles Theedam and his wife Eliza. They employed 4 men and 1 boy to help them work 153 acres. Their family included a 14-year-old stepdaughter and three much younger children. The last call was at Parsonage House, no more than a rather dilapidated cottage, rented out to the Harveys, Samuel and Sarah, 61 and 54 respectively with two children and three grandchildren in the house with them on that day.

So we know for a fact that there were only five inhabited houses in Frinton at that time and that the Battery House, empty at the time, was still in existence. Ten years later we find that it was occupied again - as a very handy residence for the coastguard George Sherell with Alice his wife and a family of four children aged from one to ten. In July, 1863, it was up for auction as a double tenement with the six acre 'Boatfield'.

Over the ten years between the Censuses of 1851 and 1861 the parish and its buildings, church, houses and farms remained very much the same. That certainly cannot be said about the residents. While Richard Stone remained at the Hall, John Butcher, 33, quoted as an 'agricultural labourer' rather than as a farmer, had taken over Frinton Wick, together with his wife Caroline, six children aged from two to ten and a lodger, William Howard. William Sallows and Catherine his wife, aged 41 and 34 respectively, are shown living in the house in Frinton Road where the younger Martin Sallows had lived. Their neighbour, John King, with wife Sarah and four children, was also a recent immigrant. The Firmins, the Harveys, the Hayhoes, the Dillersons, the Rivers and the Dissenting Minister, John Phillips had all moved on or died. It is hardly likely that all these families were out of the parish on the day the Census was taken.

Newcomers include John James and his wife Sarah aged 61 and 66, living next door to another old pair, John Brackenbury and his Martha. Next door again there lived Betsey Brackenbury with two children. Her husband, a warrener, was not at home at the time. William Hemmings and Mary had a 19-year-old lodger with the unusual name of Gentrey Bare. James Cooper, 25, a brickmaker, had a wife, Caroline, 22, who is the only woman in the parish to be shown following her own profession, that of dressmaker. John Cooper, probably James's father, also a brickmaker, had another three children still at home aged between nine and thirteen. George Snare was a farmer employing two men and boy; James Snare, surely a relation, was a 62-year-old lodger with John and Jane where his weekly contribution must have been a great help to the income of an agricultural labourer. The list closes with Samuel Rowland, his wife Hannah and their three children. So we have a population count in 1861 of 60, of whom 32 were adults over 18 and 28 were children. A small growth in the population of the hamlet can be discerned.

There are other sources to help us fill in the ten years between the Census reports. For examples on the page of the parish register preceding 1750 Richard Stone, the Churchwarden, found space to write:

"In Memory of Francis Vyvyan Luke, M.A., 57 yrs. rector of this psh. of Frinton aet. [i.e. aged] 81 yrs. & of Agnes His beloved Wife she fell asleep in Christ Sepr. 1852 aged 47 yrs. having imprudently sat on the wet sand at Yarmouth (with the Casting of Wr. upon her) which caused her death at the Weeks end."

Then follows a long epitaph which the Churchwarden may have copied from the monument. It begins:

"Pilgrims who wander thro' this Vale of Tears
Say - who can trust in youth of blooming years -
See How Life's fairest Prospects fade away
When care & grace & Elegance decay ...

Since the Rector and his wife did not live in the parish and a curate took the services, this loss could not have caused much sorrow in Frinton. The report of another death certainly would have caused rumour and anger all round the hamlet.

"1868 Jun 9th. A male infant (found at the Gully by ye sea Cliffe) (After Inquest by W Codd Esq.' Coroner) buried."

Before Kelly's brought out their *Post Office Directory of Essex* in 1855 they sent their man to find all the information about Frinton that he could to supplement that supplied in White's *Directory* of seven years earlier.

He reported: "Frinton, a parish in Tendring Hundred and Union, 18 miles south-east from Colchester station, and 2½ south-west from Walton-on-the-Naze steamboat pier, contained in 1851, 30 inhabitants and 480 acres. The living is a rectory, value £150, the Rev. Francis Vyvian Luke is the incumbent. The church is situated near the sea-shore; it is considered the smallest in the shire, and has neither tower nor spire. The manor belongs to Miss Charlotte Lushington, and to E H Reynard, Esq., the next presentation to the living.

Luke Rev. Francis Vyvian, Rectory

TRADERS

Kingsbury, John, farmer, Lodge farm.

Stone, Richard, farmer, Hall farm.

Theedam, Charles, farmer, Wick farm.

Letters are delivered from Kirby. The nearest money order office is at Walton-le-Soken."

Small as the parish was it was it was still shrinking. In 1857 Churchwarden Stone wrote in the church register:

"The sea is encroaching very fast. It would not surprise me if the church has to be moved further back before many years..."

Hilda Grieve in *The Great Tide* tells how the sea wall between Frinton and Little Holland was badly damaged by what was reported in 1856 as an 'unusual violence of the sea', which rushed in and flooded a considerable area. The commissioners supervising the draining of the Tendring levels were still using wood-thatching to protect the sea wall in the eighteen fifties, but after experimenting with stone pitching they thought it such an improvement that in 1868 they attempted to raise sufficient cash to finance an overall scheme - some £2,000 - but they were not successful. The landowners who had been so reluctant to pay the increased charges for that improvement rued their intransigence on Monday, 29th November, 1897, when a very high, hard-driven tide suddenly broke through the sea wall at Frinton and caused much damage; and all because, as a contemporary writer put it: "The landowners had refused to pay for the stone facing advised by the engineer."

It was at this time that, according to the written recollections of an old man, smuggling on this coast as a livelihood finally died out. I am indebted to Dr P Boyden for pointing the way to a letter written in April, 1908, by Mr C Woodroffe, and now kept with the Great Horkesley parish registers:

"Walton old church and Frinton church were stowage places from vessels at first. At Frinton there used to be a cloth hung across the church, to part off half of it for a smuggler's warehouse. From these places the smuggled goods were removed to Horkesley by horses taken from any farm near the coast or on the road for changes. Every farmer was accustomed to find his horses missing, or some exchanges in his stables, on going to attend them in the morning, and they

Frinton Church, 1842 (*from a sketch by the Revd. Lawrence Kirby*)
Frinton Church in 1861

were always well paid in kind. The Church Clerk at Walton has with others been in church on a winter's afternoons and within two hours has been at Horkesley with six horses with loads strung. Scores of Horkesley people settled at Walton. I remember the smuggling trade finishing about 1868. The parish schoolmaster at Walton used to start out with about 2 cwt. of tobacco every Friday after school hours, and did public houses on the road; got to Nayland about 11 o'clock at night, and did Horkesley and Bergholt, and another route back to Walton late Saturday night, ready for Sunday School and organ on Sunday."

Life on the farms of Frinton at this time was slow and steady. The Education Act of 1870 brought hopes of greater, wider opportunities for the children of the place, but they still had to go to Great Holland or Kirby for their schooling. In such a small place where everybody knew everybody there were no great crimes committed to hit the headlines of the Colchester and Essex newspapers. The next milestone on the way through the Frinton story must be the Census of 1871.

At Frinton Hall the Stone family continued in residence. Through age, Richard was now 60, through length of tenure and through his position and his father's, as church clerk, overseer of the poor and churchwarden they had achieved the position of first family in Frinton. William and Jesse at 25 and 23 respectively, were still unmarried. At Frinton Wick Albert Hicks was a young newcomer, just 28, with wife Elizabeth and six months old Margaret. He soon moved on again. His occupation is not stated but he kept a comfortable house, with a nursemaid and a housemaid. The Parsonage house, this time called the Rectory, was lived in now by Robert Felgate with John Nott as the nearest neighbour on the one hand and George Sutherwood on the other. Between them they mustered ten children and more might be expected. We see that the coast-guard had moved out of Battery House and John Popperwell, a 34-year-old agricultural labourer and Mary Ann his wife were bringing up four children there, aged from two to nine. Frinton Lodge in Holland Road sheltered William Leach, his wife Sarah and six children who had been born at Bainham, Thetford and Tendring as they moved around in search of a settled occupation. At this time William was a groom and a gardener; his eldest son Edward, at fourteen, was already a farm labourer. Sharing the Lodge with them were George Perriment, also a farm worker, and his wife, Mary Ann.

The most interesting entry of all in this Census of 1871 as far as Frinton is concerned must be that which shows 'Frinton Station' for the first time and enters its inhabitants as Thomas Humphrey, a 47-year-old 'Tralier' as the enumerator put it, his wife Sarah, 35, and her daughter Elizabeth Tutthill, 7, possibly from a previous marriage. I think the man's occupation was not properly heard or understood by the enumerator who wrote it down as he heard it, then tried to correct it. What Thomas Humphrey probably said was 'rail layer' for we see in the 1881 Census that Thomas is entered again; not under the 'Station', for that had not yet been built and no trains stopped there, but under 'Railway Gate (House)', as a 'plate layer'. The railway line crossed the principal lane into Frinton at this time and a man had to be on the spot to open and close the level crossing gates. So, unconsciously, the census enumerator in 1871 anticipated this, the most important development to affect Frinton's future. The whole population of the place at home on that Census day was only 54 of whom 29 were more than sixteen years old. Of all those people then living in Frinton only eight were born there and they are the youngest children of recent immigrants. It can be seen, therefore, that Frinton had little oral tradition of its own history to hand down.

We are indebted to one man, Richard Stone, senior, for what has been noted of the doings of the parish. His writing of copious notes between the rare entries of baptisms, marriages and burials is often crabbed and cramped and difficult to decipher and often it is the only written record of events, so we must interpret it as best we can. Kenneth Walker has been kind enough to allow me to quote from a letter he received in 1934 from Richard V Stone: "The Late R Stone of Frinton was my Grandfather and I have his silver Christening mug which is engraved "Richard Stone born February 7th, 1810." He lived at Frinton Hall practically the whole of his life, died at Great Holland in 1892 and is buried next the entrance of the Old Church at Frinton. The Stone family was connected with Frinton Hall and adjacent land for nearly 250 years."

The writer was then living at Holland-on-Sea. One of his ancestor's more unusual observations was: "Mortality among aged people up the Frinton Road:

Aug 1878 Mary Ann Lockwood died agd. 96
Sep -   Sarah Dillman   85
March 7, 1879 My man Rex's Gr. father   84
May 24   Widow Ch. Clark Phipps   89

Another of the churchwarden's comments is headed "An account of the Great Tide 1874, March 20th." It continues:

"The tide (as predicted) rose 4 feet 6 above the height of ordinary spring Tides & did great damage of the coast of Essex at Mersea. - a Mr. Harvey of Langenhoe Wick had over 800 sheep and lambs drowned on Horsey Island ... Wm. Main, tenant, had all the marshes flooded & the sea walls nearly washed down... In the River Thames the tide flowed 2 hours late & invaded whole streets of houses & cellars at Lambeth - 9 Elms & all along the banks - at Battersea it got into the houses never known to have been flooded before. My son-in-law Mayhew's entered & spoiled his wine store & injured his furniture standing 20 inches in the lower rooms of Bolingbroke House & in Mr. Dive's flour mill. It injured all the flour in the lower tier of sacks & 6 inches up the next - It put out the fires of his 3 steam engines & all the bran etc. was sprouted. The newspapers of the day said the tide was a foot higher than any on record. Richard Stone."

Another observation on the weather runs: "The Autumn of 1880 Proved wet and stormy. Great damage done both by sea and land & a great deal of wheat never could be sown." An earlier entry leads us neatly back to the Church-warden's concern for the church: " 1868. The year our Church was done. An early hot & dry season. Good crop wheat finished by the 20th August."

Dr Hicks' *Story of the Churches of Frinton,* sums up: "Old Frinton Church. The Parish Church (St. Mary's) is the only ancient building left in the Parish ... built not later than the fourteenth century... it had a Nave, Chancel, and Bell-Turret, though there is no evidence of an ancient bell ... No attempt was made to rebuild the Chancel [blown down in 1703] and the end was apparently boarded in ... with a plain window in a wooden setting, to be ivy-covered as the rest of the Church. The Nave was now considered sufficient for the needs of the small population, and indeed this was very true, for the Churchwarden's report in 1860 and again in 1875 "our congregation is literally two or three gathered together." ...The roof of the Church was in a bad way, being (1862-1865) covered with ivy, which in the course of time displaced the tiles."

"Ventilation was little thought of, and as little provided for. In 1859 there was only one window which had a casement that could be opened; the solitary door opening was closed by a decay of the structure around it. Even after the repairs of 1869, it was still covered with ivy."

Since it was the worthy churchwarden who had planted the ivy it is not surprising that it was tolerated for so long. He tells us: "January 1835 - I planted the Ivy west end of Frinton church & January 1885 I lived to see the end covered & the Tower Arches filled with it. N. B. Very much admired by strangers and visitors which I am sorry to say (later years) have fallen off."

The tower Stone mentions was his description of what he quotes at other times as the Bell-Cote or Bell-Turret topping the west wall of the church. It had openings for the hanging of two bells but no written mention of a bell installed there occurs until 1893 when a single bell is reported in the Churchwarden's report. There is a touching little note in his account of the restoration of the church: "10 July 1879 ... Making ready for tiling ... I found my ivy shorn again ... *made me so old* - I really could not help it, for I planted & kept it 44 years with care - hope they will not kill it as they did at St James, Colchester."

Whilst Dr. Hicks speaks of "the repairs of 1869" we know that they were in fact carried out a year earlier from the Churchwarden's own note in the register: "I certify that the parish Ch. of Frinton was repaired in the months of May and June 1868 and reopened for Divine Service by the Archdeacon Ady on 7th July following. In addition to the above the Church was benched & a new Pulpit & desk provided & a new font. The stained glass window put in 1836 - R.M.S."

The roof was re-tiled and floor relaid, "... all done in the best possible manner by Joseph Grimes, builder (Colchester)", who, incidentally paid for the font.

Then follows the subscription list which has added interest to the local historian in that it mentions local people and their addresses:

"Richd. Stone & Mary Ann His Wife	£30
Fredk. Burrell Parsloe Ld. of Manor	£20
The Revd. Richd. Joyner, Gt. Holland	£10.10
Mr. Albert Hicks - The Wick	£10
Miss Elz. Barnard, Whitton Wood	£5
Archdeacon Ady per Society	£5
Mrs. Eliza Daly per [illegible] Cloth	£5.5.0
Jno. Bawtree Esq., Colchester	£3.3.0
Saml. Webb Esq., Babraham	£2
Collection day of opening July 7th	£15
Miss Rose Jessie Stone collected	£20
	£129.18.0

Stone's arithmetic does not seem to be correct, but since his handwriting is very quaint a figure could have been misconstrued. He shows expenses as:

Mr. Joseph Grimes	£120
Henry Stone Archt.	£5
Hector Jn. Tilers	£3.3 & sd. it was "well done"
	Rich Stone Ch. Warden."

We are very fortunate to have at this time a description of the environs of the Church from that well-known Great Leighs Rector and Great War diarist Andrew Clark, writing in the *Essex Review* in 1913:

"Frinton churchyard was fenced, in the way most usual in country parishes, by an oak-paling on the side next the road, and by hedges and ditch on the sides next the field. It was crossed by two or more *churchways*, i.e., gravelled paths from its entrance gates (or stiles) to the church door. In most parishes, and at Frinton, the upkeep of these fences and paths was a charge on the church-rate. In very, very many parishes, to keep the church-rate at the lowest possible figure, a penny or a penny halfpenny in the pound, the fences were suffered to continue for years in a pitiable state of decay and the paths to be overgrown with weeds for lack of fresh gravelling. Richard Stone's care of Frinton churchyard secured a better state of things there. In 1860 the church ways could be reported as pretty well. In 1862, the old paling having decayed, a new pale-fence was set up along that whole side of the churchyard.

Year by year, the churchwarden was able to report the churchyard as very ample for the needs of the parish. The addition of a fresh grave-mound was an unusual thing; still more unusual was the setting up of any 'monument,' i.e., of a tombstone or even a perishable memorial cross of wood. In 1862, and again in 1865, after viewing the churchyard in order to make his report, the churchwarden noted *only one monument and three graves* as found in it.

From far back times there had come down a custom by which the parson made use of the churchyard as a pasture-close. Even in 1860, so long as only sheep were turned into it, popular opinion rather sanctioned this mode of keeping down the herbage. But in 1860, and for some years before, when cows or horses were put into churchyards to graze, parishioners stirred up their churchwardens to protest. Thereby grave-mounds, which would otherwise have been long remembered, were trodden down into oblivion; and wooden crosses, which might have stood for years, were broken. In 1866 the churchwarden of Frinton complained that 'the Rector lets the churchyard to the occupier of the glebe' [i.e. the land attached to the Rectory, in which the Rector did not live because he also enjoyed another benefice. The misuse of the churchyard under this 'let' possibly explains the singular disappearance, at short intervals, of graves and monuments in Frinton churchyard."

Clark quotes further reports as showing that one monument was visibly in place in 1865; two years later it was said that there was no monument at all. In 1869 Richard Stone reported one monument and three graves; by 1872 visible grave-mounds had been reduced to two, and by the report of 1875 we hear that the monument has disappeared, though one to a person buried earlier the same year was still there, being described as 'one handsome monument of recent date'.

In the same article, Andrew Clark explains succinctly the situation regarding the chancel: "... Tradition had it that the chancel had ceased to be in 1703. Macaulay's Essay on Addison has a vivid reference to the havoc then wrought by 'the only tempest which in our latitude has equalled the rage of a tropical hurricane.' On 7th June, 1869, Richard Stone thus explained to the Archdeacon the absence of a chancel at Frinton:- the original chancel is said to have been blown down by the Great Storm, 26th November, 1703. What had served for a chancel ever since that disaster was *the portion of the church eastward*, that is, the east end of the nave ended by a wall which closed up the old chancel arch. This was pierced by one window, low down in the wall, not unlike the grated window of an ordinary dairy. So Communion was celebrated in rather dismal circumstances, though it must be remembered that it was only celebrated four times a year and the largest number of communicants never more than four. Communion rails were installed in 1860 and two years later a Covering for the Communion Table was acquired as 'a present from a lady' as Churchwarden Stone puts it.

In 1860 the Churchwarden wrote: "Our congregation is literally two or three, and very seldom numbers six." Kelly's *Directory* at this time said there was accommodation for 55 people and after the reseating in the restoration of 1868 there was, said Richard Stone, "Plenty of room" - and as for those inhabitants of the parish who did not attend church he wrote tartly, "Their best reason is only a bad excuse." It may be that the blame did not lie wholly with the parishioners for it is recorded that the rector had not been resident at least from 1818 until 1875 when the observation was noted. At that time the Vicar of Little Clacton, the Reverend William Green was paid a small fee by the absentee Rector to take a service at Frinton at 9 a.m. on winter Sundays and at 6 p.m. in summer.

Since Richard Stone was not only Churchwarden but also Parish Clerk he had to make all the returns concerning the proper administration of the church by the churchwarden. Here we get an insight into the man's character. Andrew Clark made a summary: "Yearly, therefore, Richard Stone, as church-warden, had to sit in judgment on himself as church clerk. The terms in which his verdict is expressed vary. In 1859 the answer to the enquiry, "Does the Parish Clerk discharge his duties in an efficient and orderly manner?" was, "He does"; in 1872 a monosyllabic "yes". In 1873 a stilted hoighty-toighty tone is assumed: "I leave this for the Parishioners to answer." In 1874, and 1875, the tone is deferential: "I should hope so." And so in 1880:- "he has endeavoured to do so for the past 40 years and upwards." On other occasions, he wrapped himself in his virtue, as the Latin proverb has it: (1862) "I have never heard any complaint to the contrary"; (1869) "I have never heard any complaint for the last three and thirty years."

Dr Hicks has also provided an appreciation of this remarkable man: "...I should pay tribute to that grand old man and historian, Churchwarden Stone, who set up for himself a Private Register, and but for whose careful and concise tabulations this or any other history could not have been written, for all other books have been irrevocably lost.

Richard Stone was the solitary Churchwarden and unpaid clerk for 53 years, 1836-1889. He was a farmer-tenant of Frinton Hall Farm, under Miss Charlotte Lushington, the Lady of the Manor. He seems to have been well read, and able to express himself with clearness and piquancy. His family had been settled in Frinton from 1776 [but there is a small stone set in the church floor recording the death of A Stone in 1728, aged 39].

He was born in 1808 and died, aged 84, on June 19th, 1892, and was buried in Frinton Churchyard. He seems to have been twenty-eight years old when first appointed Churchwarden, and resigned in 1889 some three years before his death. He has been described as one of those "Typical, conscientious, down-right, God fearing, high principled, Church loving Farmers" for whom the Tendring Hundred was for generations distinguished and perhaps is distinguished still ... the Private Register of Richard Stone reveals the man; it is almost an autobiography, for interspersed between the Church accounts, most scrupulously kept, are many secular events dealing loyally with weather and seasons from a farmer's point of view, special tides, and local matters dotted about, without the slightest regard for method or orderliness. But they were written down and the pious mind of the man was satisfied." The Churchwarden's job may have been light in terms of the size of the congregation but the same records had to be kept and returns made as in the largest parish in the country - and he had no help from an absentee Rector who put in a curate or paid a neighbouring minister to provide the parish of Frinton with its religious sustenance.

The daily life of the hamlet with regard to the upkeep of the primitive roads, the care of the sick and the maintenance of the poor was regulated by the Vestry Meeting when the Churchwarden, the Overseer and the Surveyor met to discuss the situation and arrange for the necessary work to be done. Frinton Hall, next to the church was considered a more comfortable place of meeting and there the business was conducted during his long service as churchwarden, parish clerk, constable and other offices in his love for Frinton and his fellow man.

Before we pass on to the fascinating notes by Richard Stone of the restoration of the church in 1879 we should add a line about another man's intentions concerning Frinton, though never realised by him in person, intentions which, put in hand by others, set our hamlet on an escalator to development, expansion and no little fame. That man was Peter Schuyler Bruff [1812 - 1900], who has been described as 'East Anglia's most colourful and successful civil engineer'. He planned railways, harbours, waterworks, gasworks, sewerage and drainage projects. He was one of the moving spirits behind the planning of Clacton and Walton as seaside resorts. In 1864 Bruff was at last able to purchase a large stretch of deserted coastline near Clacton village, and the hamlet of Frinton: total population sixteen. The development Bruff had dreamed of - the establishment all in one go, of a new town at Frinton was achieved, but not by him.

Richard Stone's mind was not so much focused on the future, as upon the present state of his beloved church. There are copious notes in the register recording the restoration and extension of 1879. Who suggested it and pushed it through cannot be found in the records, but there is a note in Stone's hand: "Ap. 19, 1879 The Rev. F Beadle & I had a meeting at the Church. He posted a notice on the door to the effect that he had put the restoration of it & a new chancel into my son's hands, Mr Henry Stone, Architect & Surveyor, 31, John St, Bedford Row, London and he said the plans for the contracts shd. be deposited at my House after which the good work should be begun at once & D.V. [*God willing*] finished for the Harvest Home when he wd. ask Bishop of St Albans to come & reconsecrate & open it for Divine Worship." Surely it must have been Richard Stone himself, the man on the spot, seeing the church outside his door falling into disrepair, who was the moving spirit in the undertaking. The matter had been discussed the previous year, so that by 14th December it was more or less agreed that builder Joseph Grimes of Colchester would win the contract to rebuild the chancel and other building works "as he did the church in 1868".

At a vestry meeting held in April 1879 Stone reported further progress: "a petition signed by the Rector & Ch.Warden to memorialise the Ld. Bishop of St Albans to allow the extension of the Ch. by 2 feet towards East end & a new

Chancel (on the old foundation) the old one being blown down in 1703 - according to tradition." Dr Hicks talks of the 'great Restoration' and adds, "I say great because it was a £500 job, and have yet to discover how and from whence the money came." The answer to that question is in Stone's notes, which are not always in exact chronological order. It would seem that he started "An a/c of work done when Frinton Ch. was repaired in 1879 - & new chancel built" but after the following information - "Revd. F Beadel promised £375 & R Stone to find the stone for Ch. & the sand for masons & Mr Beadel to pay for rubblestone for Chancel"; there are only two more entries:

To gathering & carting 40 tons rubblestone 5/-	£10
& Digging & Carting 20 ton of pit sand	£5

there is no further account made.

As the work went forward a kind of diary was kept in the parish register of events as they happened. On 17th May, 1879, "My son Henry wrote Mr Jos. Grimes has sent in his tender for repairs of the Church & a new Chancel all for the sum of Four Hundred & fifty five pds. 5s/2d & Mr Beadel accepted it."

Henry wrote again to his father five days later: "Mr. Grimes is preparing the stone for the Ch. & Chancel etc. & as there will be more sand wanted than the quantity given by you - you had better see abt. digging some more (as sea sand will not be used) & you had better tell him abt. the cost of the 96 tons stone with it that both may be named before contract is signed ..." Stone's men had over the previous three days, carted those 96 tons "on the spot ready for use" and "being very heavy work" Stone had thought £30 was a fair charge.

Mr Grimes obviously took these costs into account, signed the contract and on 26th May stripped all the ivy off the church, took off part of the tiling and took out some of the benches from inside the nave ... "at 3 o'clock Mr Grimes came himself and Mr Beadel met him & arranged to shore up the tower & put a casing over Mrs Stone's Tomb to prevent possibility of injury." Next day Grimes's men "turned the Church inside out" and stored away the pulpit, desk and benches in one of the bays of Mr Stone's wheat barn.

On 28th May this journal of progress tells us: "People here at 5 of a morning, removed the roof put on in 1774, all of which unsound - the old original oak beams, uprights and wall plates all perished by time & on removal crumbled to dust. "Dust thou art..." we had an illustration of this in moving a poor boy buried Chancel end about 20 yrs. ago & more ... N.B. The Tower strutted up ... for great would he Fall ..." The poor boy mentioned had been a sailor. He was the subject of the following day's entry: "29th - re-buried the poor sailor in "his boots" & as there was no Minister I performed that office myself. After the funeral at 6 o'clock A M Holborough & Son began to dig foundations for the Chancel & Jms. Brown sealed rest of Ch. wall up into tower. The rain fell in the night, the winds blew "but it stood."

On 30th May the men "Resumed digging from Datum for our Chancel and came upon a skeleton laid under the old Chancel which report says was blown down Nov. 26, 1703 - also found a bit or two of old diamond shaped stained glass ..." Richard Stone's agony over the defiling of the old church in the process of improvement comes out in his note of 2nd June: "I was very glad the architect met the builder on the spot for the Ch. is a wreck." His hand-writing becomes almost illegible as he writes of the digging up the remains of Harbottle Grimstone, Lord of the Manor some three hundred years before, and other ancient interments. Yet he could not avoid a very practical observation: poor souls, though buried Centuries, what Sets of Teeth were left. He adds that all was done with reverence, "behind curtains". He ends that day, "Dear old Church - they have nearly let you down - but Henry assured me it was all necessary to be done."

On viewing the emerging foundation trench the Churchwarden could not resist the comment, "To my thinking digging out the foundations 4ft. wide looked as if we intended a Cathedral on a small scale." His 'man', William Rex, was such a willing fellow that he helped in the digging of the foundations at half past five in the morning - "... before those lazy fellows from Colchester put in their appearance: Bank Holiday - but I told them, none of that nonsense at Frinton'".

Since stone does not occur naturally in Essex and is therefore a costly import it must have given Mr Stone some pleasure to record, "4th June 1879 - a note from J T J Hicks Esq., Gt. Holland Hall, to say he wd. send round the great stone they mounted the Guns on at Holland Tower 1809 to 19, for South Buttress of the Church." It came as promised the next day and was laid as the corner stone of the south buttress on 6th June. It was estimated to weigh a quarter of a ton. It is a pleasing thought that such an object of war and violence should, fifty years later, find a place in the service of God's house of prayer, and peace.

Poor Richard's own fears were exacerbated by the comment of a friend who came to look and stayed to tea. He said he was "...sorry to see the desecration of pulling down the Church & thought Mr Beadle had exceeded his prerogative and [was] liable when called to order" But, as Richard added, "It is done & cannot be undone so I begged the masons to use all diligence with the walls both new & old. A day or two later he was more hopeful: "Mr. Beadle came; I was really thankful that he found all well, at least didn't cavil, for it is disheartening to do my best yet never right."

At this time Mr Bruff was still very interested in Frinton, but his interest in water supply was the over-riding concern. Richard Stone says, "They may get water boring at Whitton Wood - Mr Bruff was kind enough to send me a message [that] he desired to help me by any means in his power." In fact Mr. Bruff did go to the church to see progress later in the month, as we shall see.

Meanwhile, on 9th June, "Holborough inserted flint Cross in South Buttress in imitation of those [placed] at the angles of Kirby spire." After his daughter

Peter Schuyler Bruff

Jessie was upset Richard Stone records: "12 June 1879 - Scolded Grimes' foreman for pulling down the Ivy around my wife's tomb which Jessie had cultivated with great care ... telling him he could not want to interfere with the wall his Father built in 1868." Next day he was more cheerful: "Yesterday Mr. Beadel came & was very pleased with the work - and I shall indeed be glad to see it all roofed in from the present showery weather tho' that is better than frost would be." By 19th June Richard made one of his rare religious jokes. With the walls rising fast, and Grimes promising to start on the roof the following week, "I said it strikes me yr. East End is full nigh!"

Next day, "Mr Beadel our Rector came & rode round the Ch. & seemed to wish me to admire it, which I constantly did. I said I hoped the Walnut Tree wd. not interrupt the light at the Chancel window nor obliged to be cut down ... for I planted it in 1864... " the Rector said that he hoped Richard and his son and daughters would go to his place at Holland Lodge for luncheon and to meet Mr and Mrs Bruff. Both the Rector and Mr Bruff were at the church observing progress on 27th June. A couple of days later, believe it or not, Mr Hicks came round and asked if he could have his stone back. Richard had to tell him that it was now part of the foundation of the south buttress. They had finished that and were now working on the northwest buttress. On 1st July they had a 'grand day at the Church getting on the roof'.

On the 6th of July the gilt was rather taken off the gingerbread when "Mr & Mrs Chas. Hicks came & took survey of the roof of the Church & said he thought Grimes had put more timber into it than any occasion for, but I do not say so - all I say I shall be glad & thankful to see it made ready for Divine Service again, for Sunday without a service 6 weeks in succession is not like Sunday at Home for me and my dear Children. - R. S."

Two days later there was a ceremony which must have reassured Mr Stone that the restoration was well on its way to completion: "Foundation stones to memorise Window laid - present - Mr & Mrs Beadle & their 3 sons, Mr & Mrs Bruff, Mr Richard Stone & his daughter, Jessie, Mr Robert Baker & his daughter Ada from Lymington, Mr Henry Baker & his daughter & we all read and joined in the 84th psalm ["O, how amiable are thy dwellings: thou Lord of hosts!]. With us the Rev. W Green, Vicar, Lt. Clacton. Lunch'd afterwards at Holld. Lodge with the above, my son Wm. & others. I forget to say Mr P S Bruff asked me to allow him to remove the stained glass window in the west end, placed there by my Wife & myself in 1840. I said Yes - put it over Mr Joyner's benches."

The weather had been against the workmen for weeks. On 9th July it was so wet, windy and cold that they just had to give up any idea of work. Richard Stone notes: "Altogether the most extraordinary season in my 63 years."

Two days later the sun came out for the first time that month and the men were able to make ready for the retiling. Next day Richard was in ebullient mood: "7th week preparing and restoring our Little Church & new Chancel at Frinton, which I hope will last 1000 years, & at noon they left after my giving them a bunch of roses for their sweethearts and wives." More problems loomed, however and it was set down that on 17th July "My son had a serious talk with Holborough abt. keeping out the rain between the nave & Chancel & gave his advice on the subject to Mr Jos. Grimes; it was done in a friendly way after which my son Harry met Mr Beadel & him at the Church when it was finally resolved to move the West Window to the South, which I am sorry for as my late Wife & I placed it there in 1836. Next day Holborough began the tiling, "... I hope it will keep the rain out as well as his father did in 1868 when it was done before."

Another grim joke was made in the afternoon of 19th July when Canon Joyner and his sister came to look over the work and asked if all would be ready by 15th August as Mr Beadel had predicted. "... I said the 15th Sepr. wd. be nearer - He had been up the Rhine for health, but he hadn't found it." The weather turned bad, it was still raining on 21st July and Mr Stone claimed that the crops had never ripened so late since 1816. On July 30th the Churchwarden expressed a little homespun philosophy - "Raised the Chancel Arch - & took down remainder of the Old, my old Gothic Porch - wh. I suppose was necessary, yet I was sorry to see the old porch demolished: I shd. really think it has stood 350, perhaps 400 years or more - the new one will not be so strong or stand so long- However time finds us all out, there is an end of it."

The end was in sight. In the first week in September Grimes' men worked from 5 a.m. to 10 p.m. to get the church ready by 7th September everything is well done - no expense spared & May God send His best blessing upon it."

So we read the last words of the restoration diary: "The Church reopened for Divine Service at 6 p.m. - a good congregation & collection made of £3.5s.0d. & Mr Beadel announced there was yet due for Church - £50." At the end of the month Richard Stone added that Mr Beadel told him the church cost £500 and that he paid the architect (Richard's son) £29. All this work and worry, and all this expense, and all for a congregation which rarely totalled more than half a dozen. But times were changing!

CHAPTER 6

That church restoration which must have been considered by Churchwarden Stone as the greatest event in Frinton's history over seven hundred years was almost immediately eclipsed by a development which was to change Frinton totally and in controvertibly - the coming of the railway. The seeds of the growth of Frinton were sown many years before the new town bloomed beside the sea. The railway had been laid from London to Colchester by 1843, but the more remote area of the Tendring Hundred remained undisturbed and unconnected. By 1859 the Tendring Hundred Railway Company had been formed, and its first project was to run a line to Wivenhoe from the Hythe, Colchester, goods station. By 1863 the Company had obtained permission to run a passenger service to Walton on an extension of the line. So it was that we could read in the 1871 Census of a 'rail layer' renting a house in Frinton where he lived with his family.

Though he and his mates were laying the lines from 1863 it was not until May 1867 that the first train, passing Frinton without stopping, arrived at Walton. The railway crossed the two lanes which gave access to Frinton. Jeremy M Russell explains the situation in *100 Years of Frinton Railway*: "The railway line cut across two lanes as it passed inland of Frinton; these were negotiated with level crossings, one on the site still used at the top of Connaught Avenue, and the other, providing access from Kirby Cross, crossed by the present day Esso garage. The line of this cart track is still visible in the form of a private access road to the Tendring Hundred Water Company's property, with its prominent water tower erected in 1902. After a few years the Kirby Cross road was redirected along the northern boundary of the railway to join the Walton Road (now Elm Tree Avenue), and the level crossing west of the station was abandoned. It is interesting to speculate upon the difference a road bridge at this spot would have made to subsequent traffic congestion within Frinton. Nevertheless, in the mid 1860's it was the crossing leading from Frinton to what was then the main road from Walton to Colchester, passing through Kirby-le-Soken, which was considered the more important thoroughfare and had the crossing keeper's cottage and the groundframe levers built next to it."

It is a fact that of all the adults over 18 shown in the 1881 Census only two were actually born and grew up in Frinton. They were William, 39, and Jessie, 38, children of that old Frinton stalwart, Richard Stone, now a 70-year-old widower, farming his 200 acres and still employing eight men and four boys on Hall Farm - the largest employer in the parish. This year of 1880 had been sad for him; on 13th January his daughter Rose died in her thirty-fifth year and his grandson Henry, just a year old, died on 5th June. In 1887 he stood over the grave of his son, William, buried on 30th April, by which time Richard had been Churchwarden and Parish Clerk for 51 years. In 1885 he wrote a note about the walnut tree he had previously mentioned in his diary of the church restoration: "The walnut tree I planted [16th February 1870] is alive in 1885 but salt air does not suit the walnut & the wood made in summer generally dies in winter and never in leaf late ..." The continued absence of the Lord of the Manor of Frinton Hall, where Richard lived and farmed, is shown by the note of 7th July, 1883: "Wm. Hazard Esq. Ld. of the Manor Died at Harleston Norfolk of Paralysis of the brain - aged 55 years."

The 1881 Census shows that Frinton Wick had seen its better days. From being such a headache for Mrs Firmin, then briefly occupied by the Hicks family, it was divided into tenements housing three agricultural labourers and their families including eleven children. All the working men of Frinton were such labourers except Alfred Felgate, a 19-year-old stonemason's labourer and Thomas Humphrey, a 56-year-old platelayer who had been born in Berkhamsted and came here with his wife, Sarah, and their nine-year-old daughter, Eliza, shown as living at the "Railway Gate (House)".

We read of Mrs Mary Popperwell living in Battery House, a widow at 39, with five children to bring up. Fortunately her sons Frederick, 14, and William, 11, were already out to work as farm labourers, but she must have found it very hard to raise the money for her husband's burial. The cost of this sad occasion is demonstrated by an account entered in the parish register by the indefatigable Richard Stone of the burial of one Harry Popplewell, surely a relative, although it cannot now be proved:

"Harry Popplewell buried at Frinton Nov. 17, 1884
Revd. F Beadel - Rector Pd. him 2/6
Richd. Stone Ch. Clerk recd. 2/6
H Lott Digging grave 1/0 & burying the body
2 Young Griggs 6d each for bearing & G Sutherwd. 6d
I also recd. 6d helping carry in & out the Ch.
R Stone.

Frinton could hardly be said to be a thriving hamlet at this time, for over the ten years since the previous census it had only increased its population by one, to just 55 men women and children.

The railway had a remarkable effect upon the development of Frinton from this time onwards, as was clearly shown by a report in the *Essex County Standard* of 2nd May, 1885:

"FRINTON AS A WATERING-PLACE AND SEASIDE RESORT

Many of our readers must often have noticed when travelling to Walton by rail, the first sight of the sea, and the pretty scene, with the hills rising to the N.E. and S.W., covered with luxuriant vegetation, and the railway below, midway between Kirby Station and Walton-on-Naze. The Gate-house at Frinton Crossing is a well-known object. Frinton Church, noted as one of the very smallest in

England, is always a favourite resort. The village itself consists of about a dozen houses, inhabited by about four dozen people, all told. The chief houses are The Hall (the residence of Mr. Stone) and the Wick. The Rector of the parish is the Rev. Frank Beadel, the value of the living being £200 per annum. The acreage of the parish is 420, mostly under cultivation. The beach is similar in many respects to that of Walton, affording excellent facilities for bathing.

Situate about two miles from Walton-on-Naze, and about five from Clacton-on-Sea, enjoying the same aspect, it is destined to become a bond of union between these watering-places, and as an adjunct to Walton, important not only as likely to assist in securing improved train service, but stimulating the industries and tending to elevate the social status of the neighbourhood. The whole of the parish of Frinton, with the exception of a few acres at the landward extremity, has been purchased by the Marine Land and Investment Company of Clacton-on-Sea, and, 72, Bishopsgate Street, City, of which Mr Harman is Managing Director. His efforts in the successful development of Clacton-on-Sea are too widely known to need further mention, and there is every reason to believe the work of converting Frinton into a fashionable marine resort will be carried on with energy under his management. The Company are about laying out their new possession in an attractive form, and more in the villa style than anything that has yet been attempted on this coast. There is to be a new Railway Station at Frinton Gate, where passengers to Walton will deliver up their tickets, instead of, as at present, at the ticket platform at Walton, so that no extra stoppage will take place on the down journey.

A carriage drive is to be made in continuation of the present roadway leading from Walton Railway Station to the South Cliffs, 80 ft. wide , passing through the premises of Burnt House Farm to Pole Barn Lane, and joining the new Marine Parade in the parish of Frinton."

Perhaps it was this announcement which led the Reverend Frank Beadel to dream of a further improved church. He told Richard Stone that he planned to build a vestry and a bell tower and to put a window in the north wall. Stone confided to his diary "... the north wall - of 700 years standing!" He told the Rector, "It would make the Church look like a lantern"!

Kelly's *Directory of Essex* for 1886 was very up to date with its information on Frinton. After the usual historical and topographical preliminaries it shows that Peter S Bruff had purchased Frinton Hall and its lands in the Lordship of the Manor by naming him as the patron of the living - the man who had the right to appoint the Rector. So we have proof of Bruff's interest in acquiring the whole of Frinton for development, though he was not able personally to put that process in hand. The *Directory* goes on: "The land in this parish having been purchased by a building company is being laid out with the view of converting it into a first class marine estate, with about 1½ miles of sea frontage, half of which has a beach of fine sand gently sloped and admirably suitable for bathing; from the other half, which is less sandy, rise cliffs over 50 feet in height, whence extensive sea and land views can be obtained: the roads, varying from 45 to 70 feet in width, with houses set well back, are so laid out that nearly all the residences will command a sea view: it is proposed to form a tidal basin, cricket and pleasure grounds and a pier, to be situated exactly opposite the church a complete drainage system is also to be prepared; Mr R T Wreathall, P.A.S.I. of 30 Walbrook, has been entrusted with the laying out of the scheme and is acting as surveyor to the estate ... the population in 1881 was 30." Schools were still only available at Great Holland and Kirby.

Within a year the new owners of the land that we call Frinton, the Marine Land and Investment Company had completed their development plans. By 1888 the water supply had been provided and the railway station had been built.

The latter was a joint effort; the Company's engineer, A Johnson, levelled the site and provided the platform while the facilities, booking office, waiting rooms and offices, were erected by F Dupont of Colchester. The first public train journey stopping at the station was on Sunday, 1st July, 1888. That day some 25 people disembarked to see what was going on in Frinton and fifteen tickets were bought by Frinton people for the outward journey. Next day the company's directors used the train to travel here for a meeting of investigation and approval of the progress at Frinton, including an appreciation of the new railway station. Sadly the day was ruined by rain and wind. The tour was cut short and the party moved on quickly to the newly built Queen's Hotel where they celebrated with the directors of the railway company this important opening of the station.

The *Essex Standard* of 23rd January, 1886, put another point of view of the development: "We have received a copy of the coloured plan of 'Frinton Haven' as the Marine and General Land Company wish to see it. To those of our readers who delight in Frinton as the smallest, and most old-fashioned of Essex villages, with the smallest Church in the County, this glowing plan will be a melancholy document. Frinton Hall and Frinton Church, which at present almost constitute Frinton, are, in this plan, two small specks, scarcely perceptible amidst the richly coloured expanses of terraces, squares, crescents, roads, avenues, &c. There is a 'proposed cricket ground' of about 8 acres, a 'proposed Tidal Basin', 'proposed Pleasure Grounds', a 'proposed Pier', several 'proposed Hotels', and even a 'proposed site of Town Hall and Market'. The Pier is to be situated exactly opposite the parish church. According to this plan Frinton Haven will extend nearly to Walton-on-Naze, which will apparently be a sort of suburb. We refer to the project elsewhere in our columns, and it will be seen that there is a good deal to be said in favour of Frinton as a watering place ... The scheme for developing the property seems to have been well conceived. The roads, which vary from 45 to 70 feet in width with houses set well back, are so laid out that

St Mary's Church, 1891 (*photograph from Chelmsford Library*)

(*photograph Mrs T Milwain*)

nearly all residences will command a sea view, and the owners appear to have borne in mind the desirability of reserving plenty of open space ... The advantage of planting trees along the roadways will not be forgotten, and the owners of the estate (the Marine and General Land Company Limited) have already given instructions for a complete drainage scheme to be prepared...

The *Essex Telegraph* of the same date looks on the bright side: "The ruthless hand of the builder is about to invade the peaceful little parish of Frinton, near Walton-on-the-Naze. The sound of trowel and hammer will be heard in this usually quiet region, and bricks and mortar are about to be added to the more pleasing signs of rustic life. It is usually with regret that we mark the progress of the brick-and-mortar fiend, but in this instance we are informed that great care has been taken to preserve and take advantage of the natural features of the Estate, and the cricket ground, park with tennis lawns, and a fine marine parade being included in the scheme, the result is likely to cause more pleasure than regret. We hear from a reliable source that it is intended to convert this compact Estate into a high-class watering place ... The scheme for developing the Estate is a very liberal one as regards roads and open spaces; and will, we hope, for some years be a great benefit to local trade.

The first guide-book to include the details of the fast new-growing Frinton was Durrant's *Handbook for Essex*, which was published in 1887 and proved its timeliness with this entry: "Frinton. Acreage. 420; Population 55. Rectory, value £180; 2½ miles S.W. from Walton. A small parish, the greater portion of which has been washed away by the waves, the site of its Hall being now half a mile out at sea. It has a southern aspect, a fine, level beach, specially suited for bathing, and cliffs 40 to 50 ft. in height. The parish has recently been purchased by a building company, and the whole is now being laid out as a seaside resort, for which it is well suited, the country around being picturesque, and the beach being as good as Clacton or Walton. Already a pier is being constructed, streets are being laid out, and houses are being built, and before long it is expected this promising young Essex watering-place will be provided with railway communication. The Church (St Mary) was with one exception the smallest in England, seating only 30 persons, until 1879."

Meanwhile the hamlet turned its back on all the dust and noise of the building work to celebrate Queen Victoria's Golden Jubilee. "The weather was fine and the service at 2.30 was well attended. The people made their way to the Tythe Barn where about 70 people sat down to a great meal provided by Mr Shepherd. The Rev. F Beadel spoke, and also conducted the service. Sports, etc. followed and a tea given by the rector and his wife was greatly appreciated. Music and games in the evening and then the bonfire brought a great day to a fitting close."

Next news of Frinton's progress towards adulthood comes from the *Essex Telegraph* of 7th July, 1888: "Frinton, the new watering-place situated between

Queens Hotel and Queens Road

Jack Hodnett (left) ran a riding school in Harold Road in the 1930s, which closed after a disastrous fire.

Clacton-on-Sea and Walton-on-the-Naze, is now making its first serious attempt to win public favour ... all the slow trains now stop at Frinton, and the fast trains to and from Walton also stop when required, so the place will be easily accessible to visitors ... Practically speaking the place stood still for a year, and there has been no work going on. This is mainly to be accounted for by the question as to the water supply not having been settled; and had not the Company made a very great effort to meet the Tendring Hundred Water Company, things would have stood still for a very long period. The promoters of Frinton, however, realised the importance of securing a water supply at any cost and they had accordingly made a supreme effort, and arranged with the Water Company to bring a supply, and the work of laying the pipes on the Mistley side and also at the Frinton end is already in progress. The contract for the necessary nine miles of pipes has been taken by Mr Young, of Skegness, Lincolnshire, and the cost of the pipes and the work of laying them will be nearly £5,000; while the work is to be completed in three months, so that it is hoped by the end of September, Frinton will have a good supply of pure wholesome water. There are at present between 50 and 60 houses and shops on the estate, with one or two exceptions quite finished, and several of them are occupied, while the Queen's Hotel (Mr Wm. France, proprietor) has been open for some time. Some of the residences on the Marine Parade are of a commanding appearance, and several little bungalows are a noteworthy feature of another part of the estate. It has been decided to form a promenade from the extreme end of the estate right down to Walton, a distance of at least two miles and a half, and already the work is in hand. This will be a very pleasant boon, not only to future visitors and residents of Frinton, but also for Walton, for it will form a nice walk or drive." The railway station is fully described together with the fact that whilst the appointment of Stationmaster is still to be made, the relieving stationmaster, William Bailey was getting things in working order.

The 1890 *Directory* of the county repeats the valuable information on Frinton shown in the 1886 edition and also shows the changes taking place in the population. The Rector now is Thomas Cook and old Richard Stone has gone from the Hall where James Harman now lives. Two more named houses, 'Selhurst' and 'Leverton' are now occupied; the Frinton Hotel is still being run by William France who has taken on the post of Overseer, vacated by Richard Stone. Richard Stone, Junior, is shown as a farmer living at Whitton Wood Farm. Arthur H Harman appears importantly as 'House, land and estate agent, carman, contractor & coal merchant & overseer'.

There is no doubt that he was doing his best to identify himself with the local community while at the same time making a varied living from it. William Gillingham was also capitalising on the development as a builder, contractor and estate agent for the houses he was building.

The development of the town is reflected in the Census return of 1891: from the first page it had already lost a little land, not from coastal erosion but from the exigencies of local government - a rationalisation it might called for the Census says: "A detached part of the Parish of Frinton was amalgamated with Gt. Holland on 24th March, 1888, by Order of the Local Government Board - this part to be enumerated separately in the Enumeration Book."

We see James Harman, aged 68, shown as a Land Agent at Frinton Hall with his wife, an older sister, Eliza Vidler, and an unmarried daughter, Sarah, aged 34. Rose Smee, 20 years old, lived in as a domestic servant. At 'The Cedars', newly built, William Gillingham, declaring himself to be auctioneer, estate agent and builder, lived with his wife, Fanny, three children and a servant.

Marine Parade features in the Census for the first time, but only one house is inhabited - by Thomas Cook, the Rector of Frinton, his wife, their daughter and a servant. The Enumerator adds the note "Recently built, 11 houses uninhabited."

Edward Wade, a retired army Captain is shown at the 'Hotel', un-named, with his wife and four children. The owner of 'The Bungalow' does not appear to have been at home on this day but Frederick Bridges, a caretaker, with his wife, Nellie, and Galin Woods, another caretaker and carman, and his wife, 78 and 64 respectively, were in to be counted by the enumerator.

The only shop - 'lately built' was run by Florence Partridge, "Grocer & Restorant [*sic*] manager and her assistant, Frances Hardwick. Neither of them was born in Frinton. Alongside the shop were six houses as yet uninhabited. Next but one was the cottage in which William and Emma Stow were bringing up six children on a general labourer's wages. Two houses further along Thomas Humphrey, the platelayer, and his wife, Sarah, were still in residence. Next door lived farm labourer John Southgate, his wife and four children; and so we come to the Gate House in which the 'railway points Gateman', William Huckle, 55, lived with his wife, Hannah.

In Victoria Terrace, 'recently built' lived Thomas Womack who, at 67, was still the Railway Station Master - the first one Frinton ever had. He and his wife, Emma, still had two daughters living at home. Fourteen more houses had been built but were not yet inhabited. Next on the list is Daniel Davies, described as 'cashier to contractor of building work', his wife and their child. Thomas Oxoe, a carpenter from Kirby seemed also to be benefiting from the work available on this new estate. The last family to be recorded is of the general farm labourer Herbert Box, his wife and three children. But there is one more entry saying simply: "Queens Rd. 1 House building". And that last word can be applied to the old parish of Frinton as a whole - "Building" . The totals at the end of the Census show 32 males and 43 females in 20 houses , with 33 houses uninhabited.

A sidelight on the sort of people who even then were purchasing houses in Frinton is given in a letter from the Rector, the Reverend T H Cook, to the *Essex*

Review of 19th September, 1893, "... Our population is small, but increasing; and I should say we have double the number of residents in the season to those who live here out of it. By 'residents', I mean people who own or hire houses here all the year round, but who come to us only from time to time."

What had prompted the Rector's letter was an argument in the correspondence columns of the *Essex Review* as to whether St Mary's at Frinton could claim to be the smallest church in the country. The editor, receiving a letter which gave Lullington that distinction, wrote to the Reverend Cook asking him for full details of the church at Frinton, which the Rector gave: "... the length of Frinton Church nave is 25 ft.; width, 18½ ft.; from wall plate to floor, ll ft. 4 in.; from ridge to floor, 23 ft. 6 in. Up to about 12 or 14 years ago the nave was three feet shorter than it is now, and I have understood that a ceiling extended from the wall plates.

Then the roof was rebuilt and a pretty chancel was added, 13 ft. by 11 ft. It is said that the chancel existing in the last century was blown down - in the latter part of it ... " Noting the increase in population the Rector continues: "We are, therefore, making an attempt to double the length of our nave, which will make the proportion better, and increase the accommodation. I hear that a report has got into some Essex paper that a lady has offered to find the sum required for this. This is not true, and is calculated to hinder us, in stopping the flow of contributions, which are much needed."

The 1894 *County Directory* is tactful on the subject of size: "The ancient church of St Mary, a building of rubble stone, restored in 1879, in the Early English style, was previously almost the smallest church in England." In the 1899 edition of the *Directory* we are informed that it was in 1894 that, "the nave was lengthened at a cost exceeding £400: there are 120 sittings." Another very interesting revelation appears in that *Directory*: "The first telephonic communication between a lighthouse and the shore was laid here." It was in the summer of 1893 that a five-mile cable was laid on the sea bed from the light-house on the Gunfleet Sands to the Capway at Frinton and soon after connected by a land line with the coastguard stations at Clacton, Harwich and Walton.

Whilst the parish church was enlarged to accommodate the increasing population there were also non-conformists living in Frinton who began to look for a proper place of worship. They had a temporary meeting place at 'Ingle Neuk' in Harold Road around 1890 and were led by Mr Langham, a missionary on extended leave in the United Kingdom, but it was the Harman family, the developers now ensconced at Frinton Hall, which played a large part in the proper founding of the church. They owned 23, Connaught Avenue, and this was the house to which the growing congregation moved when the missionary had to go on his way. Miss Partridge then took over the leadership. It was around 1892 that increasing numbers made another move necessary. We know from their first accounts, officially kept, for the year ending December, 1892, that the church had hired the Public Hall, built in Old Road, behind number 35, Connaught Avenue. Their collections through the year had amounted to £9.9s.0½d. and their expenses totalled £8.6s.10d. - They were viable!

Soon they were fortunate enough to gain the services of an independent Christian who had come to Frinton to retire. He was the Reverend William Crombie, a pastor who had already served 35 years in the Evangelical Union Church of Scotland. For nearly six years he led this happy band at the Public Hall, building the sound foundations of the growing faith. When it was felt in 1896 that the time had come for a properly built place of worship, open on a daily basis, two of the Harman family, James and J Ambrose, along with the Reverend Crombie and George Hall were mentioned in deeds concerning the acquisition of the piece of land in Connaught Avenue on which to build.

In six weeks their 'Lecture Hall' as they called it, being an undenominational body of Christians, was built and ready for occupation. It was used until 1955 when it was superseded by the present hall. Mr Crombie, valiant and successful leader, died in 1898 and was succeeded in the following year by minister F T Passmore from Stratford, having trained under the great Essex-born and London-based preacher Charles Haddon Spurgeon (1834-92). Though he stayed only three years he is still honoured as a catalyst in the further development of the church. Before his time it had been a completely and fiercely independent church, but Mr Passmore pointed out the advantages it would gain by coming in under the umbrella of a recognised evangelical denomination. The Baptist Union was approached; it welcomed this little church to its brotherhood in 1899 through a deed of trust which arranged the legal adoption of Frinton Free Church.

The Reverend S H Wilkinson, another student from Spurgeon's famous college, followed Mr Passmore. Mr Wilkinson's leadership, and the expansion of the new Frinton, brought about such an increase in the number of worshippers that very soon the Lecture Hall was not big enough to meet all the requirements of Sunday services and mid-week activities. In December, 1903, a building Committee was set up to consider possibilities of expansion or re-siting. In the end they were most fortunate in being able to buy, for £220, the adjoining plot, giving an extra 25 feet frontage to Connaught Avenue. The work of rebuilding could go ahead! It was not quite so simple as that; for the next eleven and a half years the committee dealt with problem after problem - and overcame them all. The ceremonial laying of the foundation stones took place on 15th August, 1911. But the committee had been too ambitious and, although the collection at that ceremony was more than £300, the cash needed for the completion of the whole church was not forthcoming. 23 years were to pass before the dream was realised - at a final cost of well over £3,000, an enormous sum in those days, but in the final analysis it was only the south end which had to await further funds for completion; the rest of the church could and did open on 29th May, 1912.

The 1894 *Directory*, previously quoted, shows in these few words: "The land in this parish, having been purchased by R P Cooper esq. of Shenstone Court near Lichfield," that the development company had run into difficulties financially and Mr Cooper had taken over the project lock, stock and barrel. At the same time we read, "Mr W G Gillingham, estate agent, has been entrusted with the laying out of the scheme and is acting as surveyor to the estates'

Rachel Baldwin put it like this in the *Essex Countryside*: "The genius who set the scene for the eventual development of the town was Richard Powell Cooper ... In 1893, he acquired from Bruff all the land west of Connaught Avenue, and The Wick farmhouse in which he lived for 14 years until his death, when Frinton Urban District Council bought it for their council offices ... just as Frinton was at that time fortunate in having most of its land in the control of a single landowner, so it was fortunate that Cooper chose one firm of agents, Tomkins, Homer & Ley, to develop the estates, who in turn later became nationally famous, A Douglas Robinson and R J Page ... Also, Cooper had set a deed of covenant on each property which every owner had to sign which set restrictions on what the residents were allowed to do to their sites ... Frinton's most imaginative piece of planning, however, is the Greensward on the sea front, which was donated to the people of Frinton by R P Cooper, on condition there would be no pier, round-abouts, ice cream vendors and other such trappings of typical seaside towns."

It was Cooper who was the driving force behind the provision of golf links, beginning with a nine-hole course opened in 1896, extended to eighteen holes in 1904, when a new clubhouse was built at a cost in excess of £3,000, but a nine-hole course is still available for a short game - or for the tyros. It has to be said, however, that Arnold Bennett, the celebrated author, was not much impressed. In his journal for Sunday, 28th September, 1913, he wrote: "to Marguerite's [Frinton] golf club yesterday. House the most miserable architecture, with no proper place for autos to drive up to, though plenty of autos, and as far as I know, no accommodation for chauffeurs. Whole place too small. Men's room (lords at ease therein) common tea room (devilish cold in winter) and women's quarters. Course beautiful. Shut off from sea by natural sea wall. Some gestures of men playing a ball superb in ease, laxity and strength. Women following a couple of men about who were playing. Doubtless wives or lovers, etc. Immense sense of space. Also sense of a vast organisation. But no artistic sense. The architecture I repeat, miserable, piffling mean. And a rotten little 3-cornered flag flying 'F G C', instead of a superb standard floating in the breeze. The women in white or gay colours were not unattractive in the mass, and some were beautiful, and quite a few pretty. Certain matrons also very agreeable." It would seem that Mr. Bennett had more of an eye for the ladies than for the links.

This was a popular if rather select golf club. By 1899 it had a membership of 200. Yet, when we look at the large scale Ordnance Survey map of 1897 we

1912 (*loaned by Mr M Herbert*)

Frinton Lodge Hotel, 1985

see that, though the roads have been delineated very few building plots have been drawn in, and even less have the hatched-in outlines of buildings which show that houses have been completed. Though the Queen's Hotel had been built in 1888 the Grand Hotel was not in business until ten years later. At this time there was only one tennis court in Frinton, owned by the Bevington family, on the site which became the Frinton Lodge Hotel, but enthusiasm for the sport was quickly spreading. In 1902 it was reported: "The Lawn Tennis Club has a private ground, adjoining the golf links, with 3 courts, a croquet lawn and a pavilion: visitors can play on payment of a small fee."

Education in Frinton took a stride forward when a Board School capable of accommodating 150 boys and girls was built in 1898, to be run by a school board of 5 members, formed on 7th April, 1898. Clerk to the Board was A R Chamberlayne and Peter Wilson took on the odious task of Attendance Officer. Abel West was the master. Arthur Chamberlayne, partner with one Short, was a local solicitor. There were other, private schools in Frinton before the end of the century. 'Glenhaven in Harold Grove was run by Frederick Harding as a boys' school and William Innes was proprietor and headmaster of Frinton College. Proof of the existence of the latter is contained in the memoir of M E F Baker of his schooldays. He was born on 6th June, 1879 and at first attended school in Kirby-le-Soken. "When I was about 12 my parents thought it advisable that I should go to another school and as about 2 years previously a new school known as Frinton College had been established I was sent there. I now had to travel by train, fare ld., and as train journeys for children were in the nature of a luxury I was very pleased. The principal was a Scots M.A. and there were two assistant masters. It was, to me, a wonderful time, plenty of bathing, cricket on the greensward, an outdoor gymnasium and even croquet on the lawns.

There was, of course, no 11 plus in those days but there was the College of Preceptors exams for which I was entered, the 3rd class in 1893 and the 2nd class in 1894. These exams were, I presume, about the equivalent of the present G.C.E. and were held in a room at the Royal Hotel, Clacton-on-Sea ... The growth of Frinton has been phenomenal; in my youth a railway station was built as well as seven shops, only one of which was occupied, except that another of them was used as an estate office..."

In Peter Boyden's *The Growth of Frinton*, Frances Bates sums up the progress of the new Frinton to date: "In 1887 the work was progressing well, and an important day came on July lst, 1888, when the station was opened. There had been problems, however, and the difficulty of negotiating for a water supply halted everything for almost a year. When the resort was opened about fifty houses and shops and the Queen's Hotel were complete ... but it was not until the late 1890s that the real expansion took place. In 1898 a sewage scheme was finished and by then the ownership of the estate had passed to R P Cooper.

There is no evidence as to why this happened, but it is possible that the Marine and General Land Company went bankrupt. The increasing rateable value, the setting up of a Post Office and a School Board indicate that Frinton was growing in size and prosperity."

Perhaps the last words of this chapter should be the recording on the family monument in the churchyard of the death of "Richard Stone, for 54 years churchwarden of this parish, who died June 19th, 1892, aged 84 years." What must that grand old man have thought of the disturbance of his parish in the interests of the New Frinton?

WHICH IS THE SMALLEST CHURCH IN ENGLAND?

A WORD ABOUT FRINTON-ON-SEA.

Frinton Church, in Essex, is one of the smallest in England. It has sometimes been asserted that it is the smallest of all, but this would appear not to be the case. Mr. G. Byng Gattie, of Hastings, writing in the *Building News*, says that the smallest church in the country is that of Lullington, a parish in the Eastbourne Union, lying under the shelter of the great Sussex Downs. The dimensions of the edifice are :—From east to west, 16ft. 6in. ; north to south, 16ft. The patronage of the living is vested in the Crown, the value about £60 or £70 per annum ; the population is believed to be under twenty, and at the usual fortnightly Sunday service the attendance is somewhat less. The appearance of this communication led us to write to the Rev. T. H. Cook, rector of Frinton, asking him for some particulars about his church, and he has responded n the following most interesting letter —

The Rectory, Frinton-on-Sea, Colchester,
19th Sept., 1893.

Dear Sir,—In reply to your letter of yesterday, the length of Frinton Church nave is 25 feet ; width, 18½ feet ; from wall plate to floor, 11 feet 4 inches ; from ridge to floor, 23 feet 6 inches. Up to about 12 or 14 years ago the nave was three feet shorter than it is now, and I have understood that a ceiling extended from the wall plates. Then the roof was re-built and a pretty chancel was added, 13 feet by 11 feet. It is said that the chancel existing in the last century was blown down—in the latter part of it. Our population is small, but increasing ; and I should say we have double the number of residents in the season to those who live here out of it. By residents, I mean people who own or hire houses here all the year round, but who come to us only from time to time. In fact, we cannot at such times accommodate more than half of those who would come to church. We are, therefore, making an effort to double the length of our nave, which will make the proportions better, and increase the accommodation. I hear that a report has got into some Essex paper that a lady has offered to find the sum required for this. This is not true, and is calculated to hinder us, in stopping the flow of contributions, which are much needed.—Yours faithfully, T. H. COOK.

We quote the subjoined from the *People's History of Essex* : "Of Frinton church upon the cliffs a storm in 1703 left only a wreck of the west end, with accommodation for about a dozen worshippers."

65

CHAPTER 7

An aspect of Frinton's history which developed either side of the change of the century is the growing town's relationship with the sea. Robert Malster, writing *Wreck and Rescue on the Essex Coast*: "Frinton had its own little community of boatmen who in summer took holidaymakers for sea trips and on fishing expeditions and who in winter kept an eye out for wrecks on the Gunfleet." There was good money to be made from salvaged craft and their contents.

Well known on the Frinton beach among these fishermen and salvagers were the lads of the Cook family who became closely associated with the introduction of the first Frinton volunteer lifeboat. It was David Cook who started it all. He was an old Lowestoft beachman of some renown who moved with his family to Frinton about 1900 and set up in business here as a pleasure boat and bathing machine proprietor. They brought with them, sailing them down the coast, a Suffolk beach yawl and two smaller boats, the *Nil Desperandum* and the *Nellie Swift*, which were just the right size for operating off the beach. In October, 1901, they also brought down from Lowestoft a 32 feet long surf boat called *The Godsend*, formerly a lifeboat which they used to get out to ships that went aground on the Gunfleet and other dreaded sands in Frinton's offing. Rescue of fellow mariners was their first intent, but salvage payments were also very useful for keeping the wolf from the door.

Having renamed it the *Sailor's Friend*, they straightaway put it into service through the summer for those boat trips so popular with the increasing number of holidaymakers. But even that was interspersed with sallies out to the sandbanks. In July, 1903, the casualty was the Ipswich barge *Intrepid*, and in August, 1906, they were called out to the barquentine *Lanoy*, stuck fast on the Gunfleet sands, to take off the crew and their gear. But the old *Sailor's Friend* was getting tired. Making for shore it lost its mast. The crew rigged a jury mast and landed everyone safely ashore. That night rescued and rescuers rode together in a torchlight procession through Frinton to help raise cash for a new lifeboat. Truly that boat had been a sailor's friend. It carried on down, to 1907, launched 24 times on rescue missions in that time.

The new *Sailors' Friend*, built and launched at Harwich on 5th August, 1907, was commissioned by trustees of the Frinton Volunteer Lifeboat Society with the backing of the town council at a cost of £360. Because the whole crew were strictly teetotal it was christened at its launch with a bottle of sea water. It continued the tradition of trips round the lighthouse (on the Gunfleet sands) in the summer and rather more dangerous trips across those and other sandbanks on missions of mercy throughout the year. On one such trip, at the end of 1910, they rendezvoused with the Clacton boat on the East Barrow sands to lighten the cargo of the steamship *Antigone* in an effort to refloat it. Much of that cargo

The Sailors' Friend owned by the Cook family (*loaned by Mr P J Hayward*)

Old Road, 1906 (*loaned by Mr M Herbert*)

came ashore on Frinton beach - beans and nuts and sacks of barley to the delight of a recently arrived band of ardent beachcombers.

In April, 1911 there were some ultra-high tides and severe storms. Frinton's sea defences were badly battered. The *Sailors' Friend*, called out to the sands of the Middle Swin, lost a man overboard - Cecil Bambridge, just 20 years old, a Frinton carpenter. They searched the area for 3½ hours, then had to run with the storm down to the Isle of Sheppey. Bambridge's body drifted in on the Isle of Grain and was returned to Frinton for a typical lifeboatman's burial with full honours in the old churchyard. He had served four years on the *Sailors' Friend*.

The growing township did not really appreciate the value or the cost of the lifeboat in the town's daily life. In 1914 only eight people attended the annual general meeting of the Frinton Volunteer Lifeboat Society, when a deficit in the accounts was announced. The lifeboat lost its crew to the war effort and ended in ignominy - sinking at its moorings opposite the Beach Hotel - itself now only a memory. The boat was raised to end its days as a converted pleasure yacht.

The state of the little town at this time can be gathered from the farewell speech made by the Clerk, P O Macdonald on his retirement in 1934.

He had lived there for 35 years and had been Clerk for 32 of them. "When I came to Frinton it was a small rural village with one public road - Old Road - leading to the church, and Fourth Avenue was a private road laid out by the Cooper Estate. Connaught Avenue and the Esplanade were rough cart tracks. Its affairs were managed by the Council of the Tendring Rural District who were also the Guardians of the Poor, and the only thing they managed to do for Frinton at that time was to extract every half year a very considerable sum of money from its handful of ratepayers for maintaining the workhouse and its inmates at Tendring. There was, of course, a Parish Council, but you know Parish Councils are, simply very small engines for letting off steam. They do not develop much horse-power, although they have plenty of horse-sense."

The last county directory of the nineteenth century, produced in 1899, shows Frinton still as a parish in the Tendring Hundred for administrative purposes. That 'Hundred' was constituted a Rural District Council under the Local Government Act of 1894. At this point we can chart Frinton's progress from the status of a humble, ancient parish to that of its membership of the Tendring Hundred group of parishes and its 'Rural Sanitary District', aiming to provide better organisation of water and drainage in the interests of the health of the inhabitants of the Hundred as a whole, and thus into the reorganised Tendring Rural District until, in 1901 it achieved, through its rapid rise in population, the status of an Urban District Council. Minor changes in its physical shape on the map - rationalisation of its boundaries - took place in 1883, 1888 and 1905.

Further development down to 1934 led to the creation of the one local government unit of Frinton and Walton Urban District which also for ease of management included part of Kirby-le-Soken and the whole of Great Holland. Under the swingeing local government 'reform' of 1974 this Urban District was forced to give up its powers to the new large Tendring District Council. But the parish council of Frinton and Walton Civil Parish, created in 1934 to effect their fusion into that urban district, still meets to deal with minor local matters.

Progress is indicated in the 1902 *Directory*, "The streets are lighted by oil lamps but gas is also supplied from works at Walton-on-the-Naze. An abundance of pure spring water is obtained direct from Mistley by the pumping works of the Tendring Hundred Waterworks Company, who are (1902) erecting a water tower near the railway station. A complete drainage scheme was carried out in 1898, for £4500, under the provisions of the Local Government Act, 1894."

While the directory gives an optimistic evaluation of Frinton at this time, a look at the sale catalogues reflects the difficulties which beset the development company, leading to the taking over by Richard Powell Cooper. On 1st June, 1903, "In a marquee upon the estate", the auctioneer Edwin T Gilders prepared for the sale of "45 plots of Freehold Building Land" and "6 Capital Marine Residences and Bungalows". There were some restrictions imposed on the buyers of property; take, for example, "Stipulation" (e.) "No caravans or steam circus nor any steam musical instrument, concert platform, hut, tent, shed, house on wheels, or other chattel shall be erected, made, placed or used or be allowed to remain upon any lot, and the Vendors or the owner or owners of the other Lots or any part thereof may remove and dispose of such erection or any such other thing, and for that purpose may break or remove fences, and forcibly enter upon any Lot upon which a breach of this stipulation shall occur, and shall not be responsible for the safe keeping of anything so removed or for the loss thereof, or any damage thereto or to any fence. The auction was a total failure; only five plots were sold. None of the houses was sold - some received no bid at all; others did not reach the reserve price and one was simply 'passed over' by the auctioneer - not even put up for bidding to begin. These houses, some of the earliest built in this development included 'The Bungalow' with a 64 feet frontage to the Esplanade; Strathmere, formerly Ray Garth, in Upper Fourth Avenue; Laburnham, Oakleigh and Tidscott in Upper Third Avenue and Burleigh in Third Avenue.

Another insight into the standards set in the development of Frinton is gained from perusal of the sale catalogue for "The Rock", auctioned by C M Stanford of Colchester at The Casino on Saturday 27th August, 1910, at 4 p.m. The Rock was three storeys high and had eight bedrooms. "The lighting of the house is by electricity and communication throughout by electric bells." Viewing could be arranged through Messrs. Tomkins, Homer & Ley, the local architects.

"Stipulations and Remarks" include: 2. No Beer-shop or Premises for the sale of Malt or Spirituous Liquors will be allowed, nor shall the trade of Innkeeper, Victualler or Retailer of Wines, Spirits or Beer be carried on...

The Esplanade, 1905
Harold Road and Free Church, 1920 (*photograph loaned by Mr M Herbert*)

3. THE ESPLANADE. No house of less value than £750 may be erected on any plot.
SECOND AVENUE. No house of less value than £450 may be erected on any plot.
6. The Esplanade is made up, sewered and expenses paid. The Second and Third Avenues are made up but not yet taken over."

When it was up for auction again in 1948 at the Queen's Hotel, "The Rock" was described as: "Artistically designed, and substantially built, modern freehold residence ... frontage to the Esplanade of about 69 ft 6 ins, and has a return frontage to Third Avenue of about 70 ft. 6 ins.", with ten bedrooms.

Though that sale in June 1903 was so disappointing the developers tried again on the following 15th August. In a marquee in the grounds of the Esplanade Hotel they invited bids for 100 plots of land, 8 "Seaside Residences and 2 freehold shops. It is interesting to note that Edwin Gilders the auctioneer was still working at this time in conjunction with Mr John A Harman. The large number of roads laid out by this time is indicated in the description of the properties in the sale catalogue: "100 plots of choice Freehold Building Land, ripe for immediate building, and having good Sea Views over the noted Golf Link and with excellent frontages to the Ashlyns Road, Cambridge Road, Eton Road, The Esplanade, Hadleigh Road, Kirby Road, First, Second, Third, Fourth and Fifth Avenues, Old Road, Raglan Road, Harold Road, Oxford Road, Winchester Road, Pole Barn Lane and Station Road."

It might be that the failure of the first sale was due to the fact that prospective purchasers were worried by the newspaper reports of the great land-slip of January, 1901, when a very large area of the cliff fell into the sea. At the enquiry considering Frinton's application for urban district status it was reported that the sea had advanced 180 feet in 27 years. The new Urban District Council inherited this burden of responsibility when it was constituted the following October.

By 1903 it had won the support of Parliament in the passing of "An Act to authorise the Council for the Urban District of Frinton-on-Sea in the County of Essex to construct and maintain sea walls and other works at Frinton-on-Sea and to improve and regulate the sea front of the said district and for other purposes." It received the royal assent on 21st July 1903 and then a vast programme was set in motion. A sea wall of very solid concrete, combined with a promenade three quarters of a mile long. Behind the promenade the cliffs were sloped less steeply and drained to render them permanently stable. They were then turfed and the familiar 'zig-zag' path was laid to give pedestrians easy access to the sands. Thus was the Greensward created, a mile long from the golf course along to Sandy Hook, and when it was created Richard Powell Cooper gave it freely in perpetuity to the inhabitants of Frinton for their everlasting enjoyment. Sea defences were improved with 32 stout timber groynes built well out towards low-water mark.

'Oceana', Old Road. The Jessup family rented the house from the Marshes, who had paid £900 for it in the 1920s. (*photograph from Mrs E Last*)

On returning to our chronological review of Frinton's development we cannot do better than to refer again to that valuable record of those days, produced at the very time it was all happening, in a big, bright-red volume, lettered in gold - *Kelly's Directory of Essex* for 1902. We can imagine the Frintonians of the day turning its crisp new pages to see if their names have been included, in the rather exclusive 'Private Residents' section showing 109 names, or in the 'Commercial' section as an up-and-coming Frinton business among the 94 names. Just a selection will show how the place was truly justifying its urban status.

New residents needed a doctor - there were no less than three already in business. Schools for their children included the Board School already mentioned, Miss Goldsmith's Boys' Preparatory School at St Margaret's in Fourth Avenue, and Frinton College established by William Innes as early as 1894 - of which more anon.

There was even a 'private tutor' - Patrick Macdonald who we already know as Clerk to the Urban District Council. Frank Anderson provided the wherewithal for heating and cooking with his coal depôt in the station yard and his office in Old Road. The Electric Light and Power Company, under George Collins, offered the clean alternative. Gas was piped from Walton-on-the-Naze. Four grocers in Station Road and Pole Barn Lane, and two greengrocers kept the Urban District well fed. The cycle agent Telford Ratcliffe diversified his business to include the sale and servicing of the new motor cars which raised the summer dust on rutted 'roads' around the developing township. One could get daily papers from Ada Clouting the tobacconist in Station Road; butchers and bakers were sufficiently present. A watchmaker, Ernest Wadsman, had set up shop at 3 Old Road, hoping to benefit from an influx of genteel visitors. That Frinton was a place of the future is indicated by the founding of "Marconi's Wireless Telegraph Training College" in Third Avenue. Yet it did not ignore the past in that a "Home for Aged Men and Women" had already been founded by Henry Langston in Old Road under the Matronship of Mrs E Chilvers.

Many another choice morsel of information is contained in the *Directory's* preliminary account of the town: the nave of the parish church was made longer in 1894 at a cost of over £400; Rev. Thomas Cook had been rector there since 1888; the power to appoint the parson resided in the trustees of the late Peter S Bruff. It continues: "The Free Church (Nonconformist) erected in 1896 is a temporary wooden building with corrugated iron roof, and has 150 sittings. The Parish Church Hall, built in 1897 at a cost of £450, is an iron building, with 180 sittings; it is used both as a Sunday School and for religious meetings. There is also a small Public Hall holding about 100 persons. There are fine golf links of 18 holes, the golf club has about 400 members, and is open to visitors".

That golf course is said to have its origin in a nine-hole course started by Tom Dunn on the western end of the Greensward in 1896, with a clubhouse

The Golf Club House, c.1930
The tennis courts and Hillcrest School (*loaned by Mrs T Milwain*)

erected in Third Avenue in 1899. Now it is laid out on what was once known as part of Holland Marshes, used before that as a famous venue for hare-coursing.The present clubhouse has developed from a nucleus built in 1907.

The *Directory* continues: "Within 100 yards of the links is the Grand Hotel, erected in 1898 and commanding extensive land and sea views. The Lawn Tennis Club has a private ground, adjoining the golf links, with 5 courts, a croquet lawn and a pavilion; visitors can play on payment of a small fee. The Jubilee Garden was laid out in 1897, at a cost of about £200 and contains a shelter presented by Thomas Edmund Marshall Esq., and a drinking fountain is now (1902) being erected outside the garden ... The population in 1891 was 75 in the civil and 87 in the ecclesiastical parish, and in 1901 was 644 ..." In other words the population had increased more than seven times in ten years.

The Post Office, run by sub-postmistress Mrs Eliza Smith, had by now been promoted to a Post, Money Order, Telegraph Office, Telegraph Money Office, Savings Bank and Annuity, Insurance and Express Delivery and Parcel Office. Letters were received at 7 a.m., 12.45 p.m. and 5.40 p.m.. and were collected at 9.10 a.m., 3.5 p.m. and 6.30 p.m. During the season extra collections were made at 10.55 a.m. and 7.35 p.m. There were just two wall letter boxes throughout the town - at the railway station and in Pole Barn Lane. That this provision for posting holiday postcards and letters would soon prove to be quite inadequate is shown by the large number of people shown in the directory as having apartments available, taken up not only by summer visitors but also by those people looking round for a home to buy or rent, in or out of season. John Munson made his living as a cabman driving such people to and from the station.

The town had not seen the first full year of its new status as an Urban District when the *Directory* was published, so it was able to show the names of those first founder-members and the dates when they would have to retire and seek re-election if they so desired:

Members	Retire in April
John Lyon Corser	1903
Edwin Eshelby	1903
William Webster	1903
Charles Ashmall	1904
William Robert Dockrell	1904
Thomas Edmund Marshall	1904
John Isaac King	1905
Robert George Setterfield	1905
Ludwig Sichel	1905

The first officers to serve this Council were:

Clerk and Collector	P O Macdonald, M.A., Glencoe, Old Road
Treasurer	H Weatherhead, Town Hall, Clacton
Medical Officer of Health	W H Cuthbert, Southleighs, Fourth Avenue

Surveyor & Sanitary Inspector   T W Golds, Thorpe-le-Soken
Assistant Overseer   P O Macdonald, M.A., Glencoe, Old Road

The Council Offices were first at 21 Old Road, with the large room upstairs as the Council Chamber and the Surveyor ensconced in the shop. There they met until 1915.

These days were remembered by Hector Humphrey when he was interviewed by the *East Essex Gazette* nearly twenty years ago, after fifty years in business at Fowler's, the bookshop and newsagents, which his mother, then Miss Fowler, started in 1902. He could remember the allotments laid out between the shops off Connaught Avenue, and the sheep grazing on the Greensward, the old army hut opposite the Post Office which served as the Church Hall. On the other side of Connaught Avenue stood Deyne Court and some of the earliest Frinton houses.

Next to Taylor's the grocers was the 'depôt' for beach huts and their repairs during winter months. On the corner where Connaught Road joined Old Road there was a Penny Bazaar run by members of the Harman family. The railway then ran along the line of Waltham Way and the Leas with two fields from there to the edge of the cliff. The reason for the transport of the beach huts to the safety of the cliff top can be understood when we read in Hilda Grieve's *Great Tide* that the sea wall between Frinton and Little Holland was topped by the tide in several places in 1904 and again in 1906.

Amongst all the houses and shops then being built just one has achieved national recognition through its entry in the authoritative *Buildings of England - Essex* by Nikolaus Pevsner in its second edition of 1965: "The Homestead, Second Avenue, corner of Holland Road. The most remarkable of the villas of Frinton. 1905 by C F A Voysey, [1857-1941], whose designs for small houses were a complete break-away from the sterile academic tradition - [*Chambers's Encyclopædia*] in his unmistakable, homely, and sensitively proportioned and detailed style. The house should be looked at from the corner so that the difference of levels comes out." Pevsner also added the note that at the time of writing "... the first tower-block development is taking place."

Now the pace of development was accelerating and the Urban District had all the amenities expected in such an important area. The water tower built by the Tendring Hundred Waterworks Company in 1902 was officially opened in 1903 with its steel girders flag-bedecked to the delight of a great crowd of Frintonians. The company, riding a wave of prosperity acquired the Gas and Water Company at Walton and so was able to lay its pipes to Frinton and provide street lighting of the most modern standard, as well as a show-room in the heart of the town.

By now there were enough people in the community to bring about the formation of clubs and associations where those with a common interest could get together. One excellent example is found in tennis. The history of the Frinton

Lawn Tennis Club has been written by N F Pertwee in 1975, when he was President. He opens his account with remarks which clearly show the unique position which this little local tennis club very quickly achieved:

"Over the past years it has been enjoyable hearing famous visiting players talk in a most flattering way about our Club. Some with considerable experience have said we have one of the finest in the world! These sort of friendly remarks are good to hear and perhaps it is true to say we could be in the top twenty with our tennis facilities."

The club was formed late in 1900 by the Bevingtons, who owned the only tennis court in Frinton at that time and their friends, including Mrs Franklin. They leased the land from the Cooper Estate. It has expanded outwards from that first section, for which they paid the princely rent of £6 a year, and so gave birth to "The Frinton Lawn Tennis, Croquet and Bowls Club." It was not three years old when it held its first open tournament, getting entries from half the county. It was such a successful venture that it developed as the President said, "into a tournament of worldwide significance with a number of Wimbledon winners featuring on the winners list."

In 1908 one could count no less than nineteen courts in continuous use through the season. Even in 1914 the tournament was organised and successfully concluded just a few days before war was declared. The moving spirit at this time was the new Secretary Percy J Bangs. He ran that tournament and through the war did everything he could to keep the club alive. He even cut the grass by hand! The famous novelist and journalist Ursula Bloom remembered the kindness of this man and his wife who were running the White House Hotel when she came to live in Frinton. The hotel stood on the corner of Harold Road and Connaught Avenue. During World War II it was damaged beyond repair by bombing, so it was demolished and after the war was rebuilt much smaller.

Norman Pertwee has laid out a complete chronology of the Club's progress through the years. We will therefore only touch in the highlights. The hard courts laid in 1919 and used until 1975 were built on the area north of Ashlyns Road given up by the Golf Club in 1909 in its reconstruction and realignment of the course. In 1911, when the subscription was just a guinea, further lease from Cooper Estates took the Club on to 1924. In the days before the Great War it had no bar - members brought along their own bottles and drinks were dispensed from them in the house then called "The Elders", which occupied the site of the present men's changing room.

Percy (Popsy) Bang's long reign as Secretary extended twenty years until his retirement in 1935. He died shortly afterwards. He often welcomed distinguished visitors to the Club, including the Prince of Wales (later Edward VIII) who often stayed with Glidden Osborne at 'Marylands'. Winston Churchill and Douglas Fairbanks illustrate two ends of the spectrum of shining notabilities who could be seen in the Club where members respected their privacy and left them to their precious moments of anonymous relaxation. The success of the Club culminated in the building of a ballroom, opened with a grand party on 27th June 1936, complete with clock presented by Sir Albert Stern, a substantial backer of the scheme. In his usual self-abnegating style Norman Pertwee sums up the difficulties of the Second World War:

"1941. N F Pertwee makes use of his army contacts to get co-operation in continuing the Club virtually for the Services, and this continue for the next three years, with several matches being played and a good standard of tennis operating. Many nationalities used the courts, including Poles, Czech, Dutch and Americans. Jack Morris, the only groundsman left, but with co-operation from the Services, these were maintained. King Zog of Albania with his beautiful wife Queen Geraldine comes to a Club Dance.

1942. On a Sunday the Club raided by German Focke-Wolfe fighter planes who machine-gunned players, fortunately without casualties. (N F Pertwee, facing the sea wall, was first to see them as they came over, and he hit the ground). (He was playing tennis with two Poles and a Czech).

1943. A. G. M. only. The Cooper Estate had waived rent for the duration. Emperor of Abyssinia and entourage visited the Club ...

1946. Slazengers were seeking old balls for renovation. The flagpole cannot be removed from its present socket as it is surrounded by live mines ... Gin heavily rationed and quantities reduced for dances. Tank traps surround the Club..."

The end of that era was marked by the death of Sir Richard Cooper, the President.

The fiftieth anniversary of the Club was celebrated on 17th August, 1949, with a "Special dance and Club competitions, and a large cocktail party with military band, to which 250 people came." In 1953 the coronation of Queen Elizabeth II was the reason for a great co-operative effort with the golf, cricket and war memorial clubs in the staging of a Grand Dance. The standing of the Tennis Club was clearly shown in the following year on the death of the president, the Marquis of Abergavenny, for he was succeeded by the Earl of Cottenham. That reputation was also shown at the Open Tournament of 1970 when Mrs Jones, the 1969 Wimbledon champion, was matched against Mrs Court the 1970 Wimbledon champion. The latter was the conqueror here at Frinton.

In 1909 the club historian records, incidentally, of the golf club area north of Ashlyns Road: "Currently only two houses in this area appeared to be 'Homestead' and 'Hillcrest', Second Avenue, pulled down in 1972." The demolition of Hillcrest certainly was the end of a chapter, for it had started before the end of the nineteenth century as the first preparatory school in Frinton. It was called Frinton College, started just prior to 1894 by William Innes and shown in the 1899 *Directory* as a private school still run by him. By 1906 the Principal is shown

Connaught Avenue, 1906 (*loaned by Mrs T Milwain*)

Sterndale High School (Headmistress Miss Gilbert), Harold Way, c.1927. (*photograph loaned by Mr Mervyn Herbert [3rd from right, front row]*)

as K Stuart, B.A. and the address as Hadleigh Road. In 1910 it further reports: "Frinton College, a high-class boarding school for boys, in commanding situation, was built in 1907."

We have another source of information on the school - Simon Dewes, well known for his autobiographical recollections of life in Suffolk. He was there as pupil and master and remembers that the first school he attended "was a preparatory school named Hill Crest, at Frinton-on-Sea." His mother had made arrangements with Mrs Stuart, the Headmaster's wife and Simon was to begin on 24th September, 1919. That year the boys had been granted an extra week's holiday to mark the signing of the treaty which officially ended the Great War. In a visit some years before by horse and trap a very young Simon had seen "a rather grim, red-brick building, which had been built by Mr Stuart about ten years earlier" which "looked extremely like a prison and not a particularly comfortable one at that ... Mr Stuart was a Scotch Presbyterian of the most narrow and bigoted persuasion." He valued the education he received there but as a boy brought up in an ancient country town he felt out of place, "... for Frinton was an entirely new town ... no crooked streets and alleys ... no market, no Town Hall, no pub, though there were some enormous hotels ... The only ancient building that I ever discovered - and that was years later when I went back to Hill Crest as a Master - was the tiny church, which had been ruined by having a hideous temporary extension added to it ... "

He did find some friends in the sweet shops where he spent his pocket money, remembering the kindness of Mrs Shaw, who kept a small shop in Connaught Avenue, and Mrs Faiers who struggled but failed to eke out a living from her tiny shop. His love of horses brought him into happy association with the grooms at Race and Scott's livery stables. He makes the point that, of all the acquaintances made while at school only one, Mrs Shaw's husband, could claim to have been born in Frinton. "... When I came to Frinton the whole place, as it existed was less than 20 years old." He explains how Mr Stuart had moved what was technically his wife's school from Ipswich to Frinton in 1906, on a site bought from the estate owned by Sir Richard Cooper then being developed. Simon Dewes describes school life so graphically that one must refer the reader to his *Essex Schooldays* for the details. It was not an easy life but "Through Mr Stuart's teaching boys won scholarships to all the major public schools."

Let us leave Simon with a last memory of Frinton in the twenties. He had a cycle accident in Connaught Avenue and was picked up, with no more than a graze, by none other than the world-famed actress Gladys Cooper [1888-1971] who favoured Frinton as a refuge from the inevitable media exposure.

Having extended the history of the College, for the sake of continuity, we now return to the general history of Frinton from 1906. The amenities provided by the developers and the Urban District itself were now numerous.

Gas lighting, a good supply of water to the tower reservoir by the station, electric light and power well on its way - Frinton was feeling proud of its new status. Religious life expanded with the erection of a Wesleyan Methodist chapel in 1903, sufficient to seat 200 people. The golf club now had about 500 members using a new clubhouse built in 1905. The main street, called Station Road when the railway reached out to Frinton, was re-named Connaught Avenue and opened as such by H.R.H. the Duchess of Connaught on 16th September, 1904. The Duke and his wife had been staying at the Grand Hotel in the course of supervising the combined army and navy manoeuvres that year at Clacton. By 1910 it could be reported that the Plymouth Brethren had moved into their own premises in Old Road, and the Masons, too, had their own Hall by 1908, all nice and neat in warm red brick at a cost of £800 or so.

Station Road, Frinton-on-Sea.

Station Road, 1905

CHAPTER 8

That Frinton had truly attained the status of a resort is proved by a newspaper report in 1912: "Frinton was well filled during the period covered by the August bank holiday, and the visitors enjoyed the delights of the bathing and promenading, and the golf links were very largely patronised. The figures of passengers to Frinton for the five days were:

	1912	1911
Thursday	860	505
Friday	666	648
Saturday	744	593
Sunday	253	259
Monday	445	

The figures of last August Monday are not available for comparison, but they were rather less."

The influx of holidaymakers was not always agreeable. At the meeting of the Urban District Council in that same August Councillor Dockrell complained about being rudely woken on the previous Sunday morning by the strains of a military band passing along the front. It was explained that this was an enthusiastic rendering by a company of the Boys' Brigade marching to church from their summer camp under canvas on the cliffs between Frinton and Walton.

Councillor Fenwick was heard to observe "We had a far greater nuisance in the place this week ago - a monkey, which so frightened a horse that it had to be killed." In those days it was not unusual for a man to have a monkey to do tricks to entertain the trippers and relieve them of their small change. In passing a cart the monkey bit the horse which bolted in a terrifying manner, colliding with other vehicles and seriously injuring itself.

Frinton as seen in 1913 has been described for us by the Reverend Andrew Clark, the same man who summed up the history of the place between 1849 and 1899 in Chapter 5. He points out that considerable erosion was still taking place except where the proper sea defences had been built, explains the geological reasons and then touches on the old buildings still remaining amidst all the new houses, shops and roads; "Frinton Hall is an old-fashioned brick dwelling-house, of eighteenth century type, on the north edge of the churchyard.

It stands in the middle of a quiet old-fashioned garden and some grass-plots much circumscribed by recent houses. From its garden a little wicket-gate opens into the churchyard; and thence a few steps lead to the North door of the nave (now the door from nave into vestry). Its farm buildings were taken down (circ. 1903) for the erection of the Casino, a concert hall. its fields are built over. At present (June, 1913) the house is unoccupied.

Quite close by, but more inland, is the Wick, formerly the second farmhouse of the parish. This is now a substantial brick building of eighteenth century type, with good garden and grounds. It is at present (June, 1913) occupied, but a board by the roadside intimates that it is for sale. Its fields are covered with modern houses. The glebe also is built over.

A third, smaller farm is now non-existent. Burnt Houses as it was called, stood originally on the edge of the cliff, and sunk into the sea. Its buildings were then set up again a little further back. A few years ago they were still extant, separated from the cliff edge by the width of a field-path. The path and buildings are fallen seawards and their locality is indicated by no more than a few bushes on the very edge of the present cliff, nodding to their fall this next winter. A house of this name has recently been built further inland."

Of the old church he is rather cutting: "...the porch has suffered least from the cruel arrogance of the modern builder. It is still a quaint and pleasing fabric of good old brickwork, and has been left some of its old individualities ... the nave has suffered terribly. It was no doubt imperative that Frinton parish should have ampler church-accommodation for its increasing population, but no modern necessity can excuse the destruction of a gem of old time such as the old nave was. The windows of the nave have been ruthlessly modernized. Its west wall, surmounted by the old-world bell-turret, has been wholly taken down. The old nave has been shortened by some twelve feet, and a monstrosity of composition-stone and rough-cast tacked on to it on the west. What is left of the nave is some thirty feet long. Its width is some twenty feet. Its walls are of rough old rubble-work, solid, and two and a half feet thick. Happily, two doorways, one into the porch, and one opening to the north (now into the vestry), have been well restored, not barbarously destroyed ... The little modern chancel is not out of keeping with the nave. In a north window it has two armorials on glass, of date not later than the early part of the fifteenth century, as I judge..."

The view of Walton people on the new town growing big on their doorstep is represented by Simon Dewes in this way: "... the two groundsmen who worked for the Frinton Cricket Club had come to join us and were sitting with us, smoking their pipes and telling us tales of fishing days at Walton where they both lived and how they would not live in Frinton, 'not if you paid me.' Why, they explained, there was not a pub in the place. There was not a cinema. There was not a decent club to belong to (though I think the members of the Golf Club and the Tennis Club and the Cricket Club would not have agreed). At Walton, they said, you could buy shrimps and winkles. At Walton there were caffs and several different kinds of pubs; and there were decent little shops where they knew what you wanted. And there was a pier, one of the largest in England, with a little train on it..."

Despite the international tension the *County Directory* for 1914 was produced on time - as detailed as ever. It showed that Frinton's population in 1901 was

644 and that it had increased almost threefold by 1911 to 1,510. Its businesses and industries had increased in like proportion. Then came that dreadful world war. On the very first day, (4th August, 1914) the Harwich Force, four cruisers and forty destroyers, steamed out of Harwich harbour at high speed. "There was great, cheering enthusiasm shown by these crowds of onlookers as our Royal Navy went out to find and fight the enemy." (*East Anglia Shipwrecks*). Frinton saw no such excitement but rather took on the role of a defensive fort as the possibilities of invasion reached a level of probability.

Residents left, an exclusion zone prohibited holidaymakers, and the military took over public halls and other accommodation, shops and hotels. Soon most able-bodied men had gone to the forces. Even people like Pastor Wilkinson of the Free Church made their goodbyes. He became a Chaplain to the Forces in 1915, and was replaced by the older Rev. T J Longhurst, who had to find his own lodgings, and all for a stipend of £250.

The hazards of life in Frinton at this time are encapsulated in the written record of one young man's frightening experience: "My first experience [of World War One] was not in fighting, but took place at Frinton-on-Sea in 1914.

I had cycled to Frinton from Kirby Cross, a village a few miles away, where I lodged with an old lady. It was evening and I had to use my cycle lamp, although kept dim. No sooner had I reached the corner of Old Road and Connaught Avenue, when I was immediately pounced upon by two armed soldiers. They then escorted me to their H. Q., where I was charged with being a German spy, signalling with my lamp to an unseen enemy. After much interrogation I was finally escorted to my lodgings by a diminutive soldier, who was armed with a loaded revolver and ordered to shoot if I attempted to escape. But on reaching my lodgings, the soldier was satisfied I was O.K. and certainly no spy."

The Emergency Committee of the Urban District Council worked closely with the military and many an order was issued. For example: "From December 22nd, 1914, and until further notice, no vehicle, horse or motorcar can be permanently removed from Frinton, unless by order of the military authorities ..." Other instructions reflected the very real possibility of shelling from the sea or actual invasion: "In case of bombardment, people will not be expected to leave the town unless so ordered by the military authorities, but they are advised to take refuge in the nearest underground cellars or trenches or to make their way to open country towards Great Holland ... In the event of invasion the doors of houses should be left unfastened and only bare necessities, clothes, food and blankets should be brought..."

The war ended; life went on in Frinton. The generation that went away to war were changed people. Fortunately we have a guide to those topsy-turvy post-war years - none other than the famous author, Ursula Bloom. Before her death

The military camp in the Great War; now the site of the Frituna Estate (*loaned by Mrs T Milwain*)
The beach, 1905 (*loaned by Mrs T Milwain*)

in 1984 she had written some 500 novels under her own name and the pseudonyms of Lozania Prole, Sheila Burns, Mary Essex and Rachel Harvey. Her autobiographical works include one entitled *Rosemary for Frinton*, published in 1970. Her connection with the town can be traced in this manner:

She was born in 1892, daughter of a Vicar and his wife. They separated when she was fifteen years old and Ursula stayed with her mother, earning her keep by playing the piano at the local cinema in St. Albans. Her health broke down and the doctor recommended convalescence in the sea air. They rented a house at Walton-on-the-Naze from November, 1914. Very soon she met and married a very rich young man, they took a furnished house in Frinton on the sea front 'with ten bedrooms and sufficient servants to fill them' and her mother soon moved to rooms nearby. By March, 1917, Ursula's mother had died and she was due to have a baby the following October. At the same time her husband, already quite ill, had been told that he had only a few months to live. She was in Dulwich in November when her son was born, but soon she was back in Frinton collecting the few bits and pieces her mother had left her in a small house in Harold Road where she took up normal life again.

Her mother had expressed her opinion of Frinton as "Golders Green by the sea." Ursula found it 'full of self-made business folk, the people who in those days we called 'parvenus'.' There were many retired business men who liked the atmosphere of the place because its development was carefully controlled and trippers were not encouraged. Access into the town was not made easy for trippers because the only road in from the hinterland was regularly closed at the level crossing gates where the trains claimed right of passage.

Ursula explains the origin of the development of Frinton in this way:
When his brother died in 1891 Richard Powell Cooper (who gained his Baronetcy in 1905) was his executor. He bought the undeveloped land then owned by the Marine and General Investment Company. He was thus owner of Frinton and of the farmland of Great Holland Hall which he bought in later to form a *cordon sanitaire* for the select development of the Frinton estate. His son, the 2nd Baronet, Richard Ashmole Cooper, inherited the estate and transferred it to his Investment Trust Ltd., so that it remained in the indirect control of the Cooper family until the Company, needing expansion, went public in 1958. but says Ursula "... the legal covenants and restrictions of 1886 applying to most property there ... are maintained..." and so the Cooper family has continued its interest in keeping Frinton the select and pleasant place it is in which to live today.

Houses mentioned by Ursula, which she called, "pompous, well-kept and pleasant", included those occupied by Ernest Moy, the coal merchant, Mr. Harvey, the pork butcher and men representing companies like Sanitas and Three Castles, the cigarette firm, which at this time was having a very special house built in Second Avenue, to be called Ivanhoe. She spoke of the resurgence of public

There vvas no sea wall between Sandy Hook and Walton. This house was one of the casualties of cliff erosion (*photograph loaned by Mrs E Last*)

interest in holidaying at Frinton while Europe was still in a state of chaos. Many luxury houses, fully furnished, were available for renting through the season. There had been some erosion of the cliffs at Walton but, she said, the locals put that down to the vibration caused by the trains pounding the railway lines, and it was the walks on the clifftops, across the greensward and down to the beach which were the real attractions. Hotel catered comfortably for the well-breeched, visitors as the roaring 'twenties opened. A man of character, Billy Brookman, just back from the war, had taken over the Grand Hotel, while his mother ran the Beach House Hotel where Ursula's wedding reception had been held and a Mr Saunders ran the long-since demolished Esplanade Hotel.

Ursula, living in a large house, employing three people just to look after her and her baby found time dragging. Then she heard of Turret Lodge. In 1919 Miss Phyllis Holman had, at her own expense, converted it into 'a hospital for officers who were hopelessly wounded' - meaning that they had lost a limb or were otherwise wounded in such a way that their future was jeopardised. She became a volunteer helper - a parlour maid, under her married name of Mrs Denham-Cookes. All too soon, though, the hospital closed as the officers were transferred to London and Ursula was thrown back on her own devices for entertainment and social intercourse.

She fell in with the fast young men of Frinton, rode pillion on the primitive motorcycles of the day as they tried to break the record for the fastest ride from Frinton to Colchester level crossing gates. It stood at eighteen minutes; to take nineteen minutes was a humiliation. She even tried it with three on a bike - the extra man, her brother, sat on the tank and dangled his legs over the handlebars. From 1920 onwards she witnessed the ever-increasing popularity of Frinton with London's notabilities. Gladys Cooper was in residence for the season at 'The Sign' just further down the road. Seymour Hicks lived in 'The Nutshell' in Winchester Road; Lilian Braithwaite and Joyce Cary often stayed with Lilian's mother in Queen's Road. Ivor Novello visited her and her children John and Joan Buckmaster from time to time.

Then it was possible to tramp the cliff path to Walton, and it was still so far from the edge that a person sitting on the grassy lip would not hear the footsteps of the walkers on the path. Alas, it has since been washed away, much of it in 1915. Ursula described how the path became a narrow lane at South Lodge, then the last house in Frinton, high on the cliff. A quarter of a mile out to sea is the site of Burnt House Lodge, yet another demonstration of the ravages of the hungry ocean.

In the summer of 1920 Winston Churchill took 'Marylands' for a holiday when his son Randolph was just a small boy, who had a contretemps with Ursula's toddler. She caught him and smacked him on the bottom, then looked up to see Winston, proud father, taking in the scene. She was so embarrassed,

Esplanade Hotel, 1914 (*photograph loaned by Mr M Herbert*)

Esplanade Hotel, 1920. The message on the postcard reads, "Just a line to let you know we are safe at Frinton and shall be jolly glad when the month is up for it is awfully quiet here. No pier, no band, just a few shops, not many people, fine place for a secret honeymoon..." (*postcard loaned by Mr M Herbert*)

then equally surprised to hear the famous man call out, "You did the right thing, madam. He asked for it." Such was Frinton in those halcyon days that one could even see the Prince of Wales mowing the lawn!

Looking back sixty years later Ursula was moved to write: "... the original village of Frinton only such a comparatively short time ago consisted of a farm, the Hall (said to be haunted by a black man), the church and what is now the Council House in Old Road In the 'eighties of the last century Frinton was discovered by the right people ... everyone should be indebted to the Cooper Estate ... they were particular as to what you could, and what you could not build... They organised some of the best club-houses in England, admirable links, tennis courts and cricket ground ... " and also laid down, "... no nigger minstrels, no pierrots ... no pier, no concert parties, no palmists and other side shows ... The old trust is finished, the Cooper Estate gone..."

Ursula lived in a house between that of Edmund Marshall, her landlord, and that of his son. "Mr Marshall was one of the pioneers and had in fact built nearly all the Harold Road and a remarkable lot of Harold Grove." She added that he was a man of foresight who pointed out that development of Frinton would mean more people - more births - more deaths - and the churchyard was fast running out of rooms for that last long rest. In 1918 he argued that land should be bought at a reasonable price then prevailing before speculators could hold out for high prices when the space for burial became an immediate problem.

The Council listened to him and bought what he recommended - a meadow in Great Holland, on the other side of Kirby station. That was the last service he could render the town; he died so shortly afterwards that he was the first to be interred in the new burial ground. What Ursula Bloom did not mention was that he had worked for the town as a councillor in 1903 and the birth of the Urban District Council and he had given not one but two clifftop shelters to the town.

With a typical wryness Ursula wrote that in her time in Frinton, through the 'twenties anyone who fell ill had the choice of three doctors, Bell, Burgess and Godfrey, and if they failed then the church was the next port of call - for burial. It was still very small, though its west end had been enlarged. Ursula recalls that Vicar Knight, though not popular in the parish, was very kind to her in her hour of need. He died in harness and was replaced by Mr McClintock.

The Plymouth Brethren had a small hall here in Frinton but were based on their chapel at Walton, led by Mr. Luff, who ran a Bible shop in Frinton. After the Great War their baptism ceremony which necessitated total immersion was transferred to Frinton. It was almost a tourist attraction to see the procession of converts making its way across the greensward and down the zig-zag path to the sea wall where they were able to step straight into the sea at high tide. Another active religious sect in the 'twenties was the Christian Science movement, led by the Snelling family.

The young Ursula loved dancing the night away with a whole gang of post-war, happy-go-lucky wild young things. She remembered 'Victors', the dance club run by Audrey Richards and two friends which used the hall later to become the Roman Catholic church. The gang came up against Mr Mango who used to live in The Gables in Harold Road, and walked about with a parrot on his shoulder. He was, as Ursula put it, 'inordinately rich' and somehow he antagonised the 'gang' of the 'fast set' which included, among others, Foxy and Leslie Wilmer, Kenny Bellamy, Billy Bangs and Theo and Desmond Hazel. One of their more unpleasant practical jokes on the poor man was to creep into his garden in the dead of night and blow up his goldfish pool with an explosion which could be heard all over town. Their silly pranks earned them a dishonourable mention in the *Times*.

Another target of their hostility was Mr. 'Egg' Harvey, so called from his dome-like forehead. He had an argument with 'Popsy' Bangs at the tennis club about the standard of seating he had been allocated at a tournament. The 'gang' bought dozens of tame mice in London, took them round to his house, Kelvin Lodge, and posted them through the letterbox. Another 'joke' one dark night was to knock on his door and as soon as he answered let off the loudest 'banger' they could buy. They even lifted the gates off their hinges and carried them across the Greensward to fling them in the sea. In truth, they were a thoroughly objectionable collection of spoiled 'rich kid' adults who should have known better. Ursula Bloom was personally responsible for the stealing of the flag of that wholly admirable organisation the Children's Special Service Mission which had an annual rally here on the sands. The 'gang' had gone too far, and that may be why, when she moved into a bungalow in Pole Barn Lane she said it was: "considered to be somewhat slum-like, after the manner of Whitton Wood Lane, and not entirely acceptable in Frinton society." We could add, no more acceptable than the doings of her notorious gang.

We can set against this account of post-war pranks by the wild, young things, the account of the true life of the town of Frinton as remembered by Mona Darvell, now Mrs King:

"I was born at Frinton in 1919 in a house in Fifth Avenue, then called 'Clovelly'. It is now a built-up area, but in those days it was all open meadow opposite, including the Campfield, stemming, I think, from the fact that soldiers camped there in the 1914-18 war. In the summer we spent many happy hours playing in this field and when the grass had been cut we used to build houses with the hay. My father was at that time chief clerk at the station. I had three brothers and three sisters. My hazy memories of those far-off days are of long days spent on the beach building sand castles, swimming, paddling and catching shrimps in the shallow pools at low tide or flying kites and running races on the Greensward.

Mr & Mrs Darvell and Mona outside 'Clovelly', 1923

Our house was third from the corner. My friend Nancy Corten lived in the corner house. In summer her mother used to let rooms to visitors, of whom a family of mother, father and two children, called Bowes Lyon were regular clients. A great fuss was always made of these people. Looking back, I think they must have been some relation of our Queen Mother.

We lived at Clovelly until late 1928 when my father was promoted and we moved to Station House - as befitted the Stationmaster's family. It was a lovely old house, covered in red creeper. It stood at the beginning of the station approach in a nice garden with a gate at the top on to the station platform. By the railway gates stood the tiny gatehouse where Jack Bright lived with his wife and son. He had to open those gates for every train that came through, and close them after it. In those days the only way into Frinton was through those gates into the main street, Connaught Avenue, which ran straight down to the sea front.

The shops in those days were mostly family concerns. Blowers and Cooper is still there, looking on the outside, very much as it always did, with the green tiles and brown paint; and Luff's the Bible shop is still there. There was a photographer called Donovan who had a studio in London as well as in Frinton. He lived here in Frinton with his wife. She had a beautiful voice and was a leading light in the Operatic Society. Halfway down Connaught Avenue on the right-hand side going towards the sea Old Road branches off. At the top there used to be two shops, side by side, both sweet shops, one was Huckle's and the other Tuck's. Mr. Huckle used to have an ice-cream barrow at the top of the path that led to what in those days we called the zig-zag slope. There were two schools at the top half of Connaught Avenue - Sterndale and Hawthorns.

My father was much involved in the local community. He was secretary of the parochial church council when the new church was built; he was in the church choir and both he and my mother were Sunday School teachers.

Just after we moved to Station house, Mrs Cooper, a councillor and Guide commissioner, started a club for young people under sixteen called the Young Britons. It was a younger version of the Junior Imperial League (the Imps). We met every Saturday at the Imperial Hall in Pole Barn Lane. It was a lovely hall with a big stage and dressing rooms. It was even equipped with a kitchen. Our afternoon often stretched into the evening, with a wonderful tea provided by Mrs Cooper's own cook. Mrs Cooper hired a dancing teacher, Isobel Grant, to come up specially from London. She licked into shape a troupe of young singers, dancers and players who did marvellous shows every year and went all over the place performing them for charity. We even managed to endow a bed at Clacton Hospital, and once we gave a fortnight's performances at the Ocean Theatre on the pier. So you can see the Young Britons became famous over a wide area.

When my oldest sister left school she was apprenticed to Sylvia Gray, the dressmaker with a shop at the bottom of Connaught Avenue, but when my next

The Operatic Society in *Quality Street* by J M Barrie
The Operatic Society in Roman costume

Mona Darvell (right) in the
Silver Ballet, 1935
(*photograph loaned by Mrs M King*)

The Junior Imperial League
summer camp, 1930
(*photograph loaned by Mrs L Foulkes*)

The Beach, c.1905 (*photograph loaned by Mr M Herbert*)

sister left school my father bought a shop called The Cabin at the station end of Pole Barn Lane. It is now divided into two shops and the last time I went down I saw that, after being a sweet shop for all those years it is now a bakery. In those days businessmen used to commute from Frinton to London daily and at night taxis would wait for the commuter train to take them all home again. Tom Wash, who owned the local dairy, used to meet the trains with a closed carriage; I can see him now, sitting up behind the horses in his tall black hat. There was always somebody sufficiently intrigued by the sight to hire him.

Many famous people used to come and stay in Frinton, most of them coming down by train. Once, I remember, Douglas Fairbanks, senior, came and we all went up to see him. I was quite disappointed, he wasn't half as handsome as he looked on the screen. When they built a new road on the other side of the Cabin, called Greenway, a fine bungalow was erected at the Connaught Avenue end. Gracie Fields' sister and her husband bought it. Gracie was married to Archie Pitt at the time, and they often came to stay and would come into the Cabin to make purchases. I remember standing by the Cabin when the Prince of Wales came by car through the crossing gates and he waved to all of us standing there.

The Greensward was kept immaculate, and so was the beach. We had Beach Inspectors specially employed to keep it so and woe betide anybody who dropped toffee papers or left seaweed lying in the shelters! They wore peaked caps with Beach Inspector on them and we kids were terrified of them."

The reference to seaweed is a reminder for Mona of the day her mother came off the beach with her and her brother. He was carrying a lovely long, wide band of that kind of seaweed by which, it was said, you could tell when it was going to rain. Her mother took the seaweed and laid it on the seat in the shelter while she put on her little boy's shoes to walk up the zig-zag path. The Beach Inspector saw the seaweed and came rushing in to say, "I'm the Beach Inspector, take that seaweed off the seat!" Mona's mother snapped back, "And I'm the Stationmaster's wife!..." Mona thought her Mum was very brave.

She continues her memories: "The Children's Special Mission (C.S.S.M.) used to come in the summer. They used to build huge sandcastles on the beach and all the local children and not a few of the visitors used to sit on the sand and sing hymns like "Jesus bids us shine ...", etc. from the leaflets they distributed. That was fun; so, too, were the sand design competitions run by the *Daily Mail*. They took place at low tide. Squares of sand were marked out, you picked a square and made a picture and a caption, using sand, shells, seaweed etc. Once I won a Teddy Tail for being the youngest competitor.

"The Church held a fête on the golf club end of the Greensward and the firemen used to hold displays there. We were very proud of the fire brigade. They had a very quick turn-out, and if there was a fire in the holidays over the level crossing we all used to line up at the top of Pole Barn Lane and cheer them

Children's Special Service Mission, 1925 (*photograph loaned by Mr M Herbert [2nd from right in sandals]*)
The zig-zag path, 1923 (*photograph loaned by Mr M Herbert*)

The Station staff, including Mr T Darvell (seated left), Bert Smith, gatekeeper, (standing right) and Mr Rice (standing 2nd from left), 1925

The Station staff in the Great War

through the gates. At the other end of the Lane there was a shelter on the Green-sward with trapdoor in its roof. A few of us formed a club. We used to climb through that trapdoor and hold candlelit meetings up there: we never got caught!"

So we have, set against Ursula Bloom's account of the dubious deeds of Frinton's fast young set, the recollections of the less sensational life lived by ordinary folk who then called Frinton home.

In 1925 a well-known enemy to Frinton's splendid beaches and gardens, the mosquito, reared its ugly head again, as can be seen from a newspaper report of Council proceedings: "The great bugbear to Frinton, the mosquito pest, came up for discussion again at Frinton Council. The Medical Officer said the breeding season had begun and something had to be done now. The Ministry had said that a scheme to wipe out the plague would be very expensive. The Surveyors of Walton, Tendring and their own council had been asked to meet on the matter, but Walton had preferred to plough its own furrow. The other two Surveyors had met, however, and in conjunction with the Chairman of the Sea Level Commissioners and himself, had come to the conclusion that putting down larvicides was a waste of money. In order to get rid of the breeding grounds they must either drain them and keep them dry or fill them in." The draining has been carried out - the mosquito is now very much an endangered species in Frinton.

By 1926 the population had burgeoned above its 1921 Census figure of 3,032 and there was just about every craft, business and profession represented in the town. The relatively newfangled telephone now had numbers reaching into the 200's. Business numbers included Ernest C Homer, proprietor of the Beach House Hotel, who gloried in the status of Frinton 2; while the Ratcliffe sisters, Barbara and Norma, at the Esplanade Hotel could only manage Frinton 5. The Ratcliffe brothers at their garage in Connaught Avenue had to be content with Frinton 11. Race and Scott, entered as 'Dairymen, coal merchants and Jobmasters', in Connaught Avenue not only had 20 as their telephone number but also boasted the telegraphic address of 'Race'.

Church news at this time made interesting reading. There is the continuing story of the Free Church under the Baptist banner. In 1915 it bought from the old Eld Lane, Colchester, Baptist church the organ they were replacing. It improved the musical content of the services no end - and Derek Whybrow reports that it was still in satisfactory use in 1990. Mr Whybrow also points out how forward-looking this church was; in January, 1919, it changed its rules to allow Deaconesses to be introduced. He writes: "It may even be thtat history will prove the birth of 'Women's Lib' took place in this quiet backwater-on-sea."

In April, 1921, the Reverend T M Bamber was invited to take over the ministry after Mr Longhurst's retirement. He was a man of fire and spirit who doubled the membership in his five years service. He led open-air services on the Esplanade and introduced Bible talks on Wednesday evenings. He it was who

Hazel Darvell outside the shop which her father bought for his two daughters (*photograph loaned by Mrs M King*)

Car on fire outside Ratcliffe's Garage (*photograph loaned by Mrs T Milwain*)

saw the loan on the new church paid off at last and the building finally finished. The new manse was built on land in the Crescent in 1923 and in 1926 a 'Primary Hall' was built. Sunday School was so popular from 1920, that its membership in the next eight years increased four times over.

The next man in the Manse was Rev. William Joynes, from 1926 to the beginning of 1934, when Dr A Douglas Brown took over. He put Frinton on the Nonconformist map when he was elected President of the Baptist Union. It was during his energetic ministry that the church site was completed with the fine clock tower, an entrance vestibule, a new kitchen and a floodlighting system. Local historians can read part of the story of this fine church on the building itself, in the form of foundation stones laid by important members on 15th August, 1911. Among them were the Minister, Rev. S H Wilkinson, Mrs Wilkinson on behalf of the 'Junior Busy Bee', Mr F H Collins and Mrs R H Dolling. The architect, W Hayne of Frinton and the builders, H Potter and Son, of Chelmsford also receive due acknowledgment.

For the Church of England the great day of the post-war age was Wednesday, 17th July, 1929. "In glorious sunshine," as Dr Hicks remembers, "the new Church of St Mary Magdalene was consecrated by the Rt. Rev. His Lordship the Lord Bishop of Chelmsford and a long history of difficulties and endeavours reached a happy culmination..." Perhaps it was with Frinton's pleasant environment in mind that the Bishop preached a sermon on the text, "The lot is fallen unto me in a fair land: yea, I have a goodly heritage." Dr Hicks reminds us that the former Rector, J V Sandys-Bird should be credited with most of the praise for his persistence in seeing the project through from dreams to reality. The split in the congregation can be read between his lines: "Equally, I think it is my duty, and I hope as a true historian, to chronicle the fact that at the Consecration Ceremony there were many regrets. For there assembled were many who had worshipped in the old Church since their childhood days; it was, to them, a parting from the old House, their Spiritual Home for many years; it was a loss to them for ever of their cherished hope that the new Church might have been a grand restoration of the old Church, and on the old site. It is still an open sore with many. Let us hope that time, the great healer, will heal this long-aching wound."

The new church has its own contribution to make to the architecture of the town. The architect was the well-known Sir Charles Nicholson [1867-1949] who conceived a long, low Perpendicular style exterior without a tower, with a bellcote over the porch and an aisle whose flat roof is disguised with battlements. It has to be locked against the casual visitor in these days of mindless vandalism, but the interior is more warm and welcoming, 'with prettily painted ceilings', as Pevsner puts it, and rounded arches and other features give a softening effect.

So we come to 1930 and days remembered by many of today's Frintonians. From the mass of printed material available to us for study we can only brush in

Ronald Hooker (2nd from left), 1926 (*photograph loaned by Mrs T Milwain*)

Connaught Avenue (*photograph loaned by Mr M Herbert*)

Free Church (*photograph loaned by Mr M Herbert*)

the highlights. The reports on local government in the newspapers of the time allow us, with a certain amount of reading between the lines, to detect the real feelings of the day. Take, for example, the report of the Tennis Club's application for an extension of hours on their licence for music and dancing in July, 1930. It was the indomitable Percy Bangs who appeared before the bench and, it seems, gave as good as he got! The Chairman said complaints had been made of what he might call rowdyism associated with dances at the Club. Popsy's spirited reply was that his club was not responsible for anybody who went to Walton to 'eggs-and-bacon' (*i.e.* overnight) parties or held them in their own houses. He did not think it was fair to put it down to the club, whose officials had done their utmost to prevent any noise. He was congratulated the other night on the manner in which he had conducted the tournament, and was given a big cheer, but that could not be regarded as rowdy." The Chairman was suitably impressed and said there was no complaint as to Mr Bangs!

The erosion of the cliffs and their inherent instability made necessary the relaying of the railway further inland, so that it curved sharply out of Frinton, then had a straight run to Walton. The bed of the old track was later put to good use as the foundation for Waltham Way, when the Frinton Park Estate was in its infancy in 1934.

A much bigger cause of concern was the siting of Frinton's rubbish tip.   It was reported on 5th September, 1930, that the Ministry of Health held an inquiry at the Council House, Frinton, about the Council's application to borrow £270 for the purchase of land in Malting Lane, Kirby-le-Soken, for the purpose of a refuse tip. Frinton's surveyor, A E Smith gave some interesting statistics - the area of the district was 422 acres, the population 3,500, the rateable value £42,159, out-standing loans £60,243 and total rates 11/10d. The Council Chairman referred to the protest from Lower Kirby that Frinton had plenty of space for its own rubbish, but he had made enquiries and declared that he just could not find any suitable land. The Chairman of the Frinton Works Committee said the proposed site only covered 13 acres and no house was nearer than 400 yards, but then the Surveyor, under questioning, rather spoilt the case by agreeing that land off Witton Wood Lane would be a suitable site - if it was not for the fact that it was good building land. Kirby people had got up a petition with over 800 signatures, saying they had already had to take rubbish from other neighbouring parishes and had had enough of it. By November, though, it was satisfied arranged to the satisfaction of all concerned that Frinton should have, "instead of the field, a piece of land over the hill right out of sight, sound, and smell of the residents."

At this time the exclusive nature of the new Frinton was under attack from more than one direction.   In October, 1930, when the General Purposes Committee recommended laying out the Kiosk Field, including a miniature golf course and a croquet lawn, Mr W Lowther Kemp was firmly against it, saying that it could well lead to the demand for other 'entertainments'; so the matter was deferred. The Council was further disturbed when it heard that the Church Council, in 1931, was preparing to sell the site of the old parish church hall "... for what was known as a 'dodgem' track that was, a number of electric cars which crashed into each other." It was in September that year that Mr Lowther Kemp, as Chairman of the Frinton Urban Council, said that the townspeople were only just beginning to appreciate the reality and the seriousness of the county council's proposal to unite Frinton with Walton in one urban district. He was reported as saying that if the Council failed in its efforts, their Frinton, the Frinton as they knew it, would cease to exist - one more place of distinctive character and ideals would disappear, and they would sink down to become merely a 'popular' seaside resort, with charabancs, trippers, band, phrenologists, waste-paper and litter, and all the other accompaniments of such places.

It would mean, he said, a serious depreciation of all property in the district, an increase in rates, and a loss of control of the expenditure of their own money. If the Council stuck to their guns and were not fainthearted, they would successful. He refused to believe that any impartial tribunal would consent to the handing over of a population of some 3,000 people and all their property against their will to be administered by a body with entirely alien sympathies and ideals. That would be the very reverse of justice. Their object was simply to be left alone. By December however Frinton councillors had to admit defeat in the face of a *fait accompli*.

Before it lost its individual identity as a council, however, Frinton did put in hand an application for a loan of £15000 for a programme to improve the sea defences of the greensward and the cliffs all along the front. "The greensward was the brightest jewel in the crown of Frinton," said the clerk, Mr P O Macdonald, "Therefore every foot that was lost had serious consequences". It was hoped not only to stabilise the cliffs but also to reclaim some portions already lost. But there is always a dissenting voice; one councillor opined that, as the money was being raised to protect revenue-producing property in the form of the bathing huts, it would be wrong to place the burden on the ratepayers at large. This was just about the last significant action of the Frinton Urban District Council. A new chapter in the Frinton story began on 1st April, 1934.

CHAPTER 9

1934 opened sadly with the death of Henry Markham in the early hours of its very first day, aged 82, but the report of the funeral is a bonus for the local historian in that it contains a list of the notabilities of Frinton at this time because Henry had been "a familiar figure in the social and sporting life of the town and district." In his younger days he had been keen on rowing, cricket and golf, playing the latter still in later life and acting as Captain as well as Secretary of the Golf Club. He was also President of the Cricket Club, founder of the Ex-Servicemen's Memorial Hall and Chairman of the Board of the Tendring Level Commissioners in the last days of its authority.

The funeral service was held in the new parish church by the Rector, the Rev. J V Sandys-Bird, and the list of mourners, apart from the family, included Mr W Lowther Kemp, Chairman, and other members of the Frinton Urban District Council; Mr C W Tagg, Honorary Secretary of the War Memorial Club and other members; Mr J Murray Brown, Secretary of the Golf Club, Mr P J Bangs, Secretary of the Lawn Tennis Club, Mrs E Cooper, Mr E J Moy, ex-Inspector Girt, Captain H W J Snell, Major E F C Evanson, Mr and Mrs Brough, and other Frintonians too numerous to mention.

One of the very last actions of the Frinton Urban District Council was to present their case, on 3rd February, 1934, against the application of the Eastern National Omnibus Company to introduce a bus service in the town, on a circular route from the railway gates through Connaught Avenue, the Esplanade and Pole Barn Lane. The Eastern Area Traffic Commissioners were told: "At the moment Frinton has no stage carriage service whatsoever. The Council objected on the grounds that it would destroy the town's amenities and that, "The constant passage of heavy vehicles would be a cause of apprehension to children and others" and that, "No houses in Frinton were more than about half-a-mile from the station, and the working-class people likely to use a bus service lived even nearer the station." Mr P O Macdonald, the Council's Clerk, brought up other objections and said such a service would be "a death blow to the character of Frinton."

A farcical element crept in when Mr A E Smith, the Surveyor said there was already a service of two motor and two horse-drawn buses which met every train and also plied for hire. He went on at length - including the fact that children played in Pole Barn Lane, causing minor accidents even though the Council had just bought two acres of land as a playground. When one of the Commissioners asked him, "Have you found the land useful in that way?" he replied, "We found, Sir, that it has encouraged a lot of hooligans, who cleared the small children off." The Commissioner said, "Hooligans in Frinton?" - and there was much laughter, as the newspaper puts it. Then Mr. Smith replied, "Yes, sir, we are not devoid of them here. Poverty will always be with us." Once again the laughter rippled

Esplanade and White House Hotels (*photograph loaned by Mrs T Milwain*)

Laying the foundation stone of new church, 1929. Sir Charles and Lady Batho with Revd. Sandys-Bird. Mrs Cooper extreme right front row (*photograph loaned by Mrs M King*)

round. After further evidence and "in view of the opposition of the Council," the licence was refused.

By the middle of February arrangements for the amalgamation of Frinton and Walton Urban District Councils were being discussed; but there was still time at the council meeting for other matters to be considered: "The Council's attention was drawn to the nuisance caused by dogs fouling the pavements. They made a very urgent appeal to all dog-lovers to take every possible step to assist the Council in its efforts to maintain the reputation of the town for a very high standard of cleanliness."

The end of an era was marked with the death of Percy Bangs on 19th February at his home, the White House Hotel. On the last day of the existence of the Urban District of Frinton as a separate entity, 31st March, 1934, the White House Hotel and all its furniture and effects were sold in 730 lots. When the amalgamation was noted at the final meeting of the Walton Urban District Council the Clerk, Mr S Nicholson wryly commented: "As we have been told that Frinton is a star in the English firmament, we ought to feel grateful to the Ministry of Health and the Essex County Council, who deemed that the Walton wagon should be hitched to the Frinton star." The laughter with which his sally was received was distinctly rueful.

Frinton people were just as rueful. The proposed increases in assessments for rating had caused over 300 objections - in other words 67% of ratepayers were unhappy with the new assessments, and many more objections were expected. At a further meeting of the Area Assessment Committee a member asked, "Why should Frinton be in a little class by themselves? It seems as if we have decided to let them do practically as they like. Why should they be treated different to any other Council in the district?" In the very same issue of the *Essex County Standard* is the note that Radiolux Ltd. of Frinton had been granted the power to take wires across County roads in the town in their installation of a wireless relay service. So Frinton was soon connected to London to receive world-wide news and gentle musical entertainment from the BBC.

Three weeks later Frinton Women Conservatives were meeting at the Imperial Hall to hear a representative from Conservative Central Office bring them up to date on current political topics. There is no doubt that Frinton people were progressive, for at the same time Miss M Kerr was giving a talk to Frinton W.I. on Australia, and "...a large and appreciative audience at Imperial Hall last Saturday when Frinton Young Britons, under the direction of Mrs Cooper, presented their delightful entertainment 'Revels of 1934'. Mrs Phyllis Mead was Stage Manager." Sir Charles Batho, Lord Mayor of London, who kept a house in Frinton, was there to move the vote of thanks to all concerned. This important man was remembered by Frintonians for another service he did the town on 1st September, 1928, when, in full regalia, he laid the foundation stone of the new church of St Mary Magdalene in Old Road. The strenth of the Women's Institute is shown by the opening of their new Hall on their own land in Fourth Avenue by Viscountess Bing of Vimy in October, 1934. It could seat 260 people.

The last meeting of the Frinton Urban District Council was on Tuesday evening, 20th March, 1934. On the new combined District Council Frinton took 7 seats, Walton 6 and Kirby 1. Successful contestants for the Frinton seats were, in order of the number of votes cast for them: C W Hayne - 572; A S Tomkins - 514; G C Russell Roberts - 426, Miss M McJannet - 425; W Lowther Kemp - 378; G A Thurgur - 289; and C W Tagg - 282. The two Frinton candidates not elected were D B McGrigor and J B Conly. The first Chairman of the new Council was Mr Lowther Kemp with Mr J W Eagle from Walton as Vice-Chairman. As far as the residents of Frinton were concerned the most important first resolution of the new Council was to reduce the general rate they would pay annually from 11s.1d to 10s.10d. Walton folk benefited by another 11d. because they had been paying 12s.0d. This had not been without some heated argument in the Rate Valuation Committee. There was also the sea defence rate to pay, and that differed between Frinton and Walton at 7d. and 1s.4d. respectively, with the 'back area' of Walton understandably being charged only 2d.

Early in May the Chairman, Mr Lowther Kemp, suggested that a pleasant way for the councillors to get to know the area of the enlarged Urban District would be to 'beat the bounds', in other words walk around the whole boundary - a walk of some eleven miles. There was general agreement and so the paper reported on 12th May, 1934: "The party started from Frinton Golf Club, and proceeded along the beach, where a member of the Press was "bumped". A detour was then made, and Holland Gap was passed, Holland Bridge being eventually reached. From there the party continued along the Brook and through the marshes, a somewhat hazardous journey owing to the heavy rain, and into the Kirby Ward. At the Hare and Hounds the Chairman "hospitably entertained the company" and "Afterwards they proceeded towards the backwaters and across the fields to Kirby Quay, where they completed an eleven-mile walk. They were entertained to tea at the Ashes Farm, the residence of Mr J W Eagle, JP, Vice-Chairman of the Council."

That there were tensions in the merging of the separate districts is shown in the point made in the Council meeting that Kirby and Holland ratepayers did not think that they were getting a fair deal over the allocation of hut sites on Frinton's sea front. Now that they were one local authority they wanted to know if Frinton ratepayers had any prior right to those sites'. But matters of greater import to the whole area were now in the air. At the July meeting of the Council it was reported that the sub-committee had not yet met 'in camera' concerning the suggested development of the Frinton Park estate, the question of a site for the new Council offices, the acquiring of land for playing field purposes and the same old problem of the extension of the sea defences.

Frinton folk still went their separate ways. The annual fête held by the Parish Church on the Greensward in August, 1934, and opened by Sir John Pybus, CBE, MP, aimed at raising the £250 still needed to clear the cost of building the new church. At the same time the tennis club dance for 250 children, all in fancy dress had prizes distributed by no less a personage than Princess Katherine of Russia. The value of housing in Frinton is shown by the advertisement in the same year of a furnished bungalow, accommodating four people, and with a garage, to be let at three guineas in September and at twenty-five shillings a week from October to March. There was still very much a Frinton 'season'.

Having said that, it must be added that there was a rapidly growing permanent population which saw to the town through the winter and revivified it for the next wave of summer immigrants. Evidence of this can be gained from the strength of the Women's Institute. Another indication of the strong social life in or out of season is the second performance of the Young Britons' "Revels of 1934" in May, which brought to light an interesting piece of local history reported in the local paper: "It was a delightful performance from start to finish. Mrs Cooper is kindly giving half the proceeds towards the sum required to complete the restoration of the old Parish Church by the removal of the dormer windows."

As early as July, 1934, the new Urban District Council had commissioned and received a report from town-planning consultants that it was desirable that a landing ground should provided for aeroplanes. Frinton lost out on this, but we read in September that, "Two more golfers arrived at the new airport at Walton-on-the-Naze." Now to a more down-to-earth subject; football had its place in Frinton's history, though it has no records on which we have been able to draw. A photograph was sent in to the local paper, showing Frinton Juniors - stalwart young men rather than schoolboys - who played on the Greensward in the mid-'thirties. The last game played on that sacred green was on 17th April, 1940, between Frinton and Walton Wednesday Club and R.A.F., Martlesham. The visiting team scorned the usual washing arrangements - they ran straight down the cliff path and into the sea to clean off the mud. Who won? - History is silent!

Mud was much in evidence at this time in Witton Wood Road, or Lane as it was then called. Harry Dow, who had earned some local renown as the window cleaner poet was a moving figure behind its improvement. It was made up - and Harry wrote a poem in celebration. One verse will suffice:

"We're a happy band of children, our hearts are full of joy,
Below the tarry pavement, above the bright blue sky;
Now we can play at hop scotch and make our daisy chains,
And when we tire of playing we can sit and watch the trains."

A projected new playing field - a much safer place for children at play - was tied up with the development of the Frinton Park estate which was even now occupying the enlarged authority. It came about in this way: early in 1934 200

The promenade, 1925
The Blagden family outside their beach hut, 1929

acres of virgin land fronting the cliffs and running inland on the northern border of Frinton, where roads like Waltham Way, Graces Walk and Central Avenue run today, including Pedlars Wood beyond, were bought by the South Coast Property Investment Company for £1,500. They expressed their intention to build an estate of some 11,000 houses - to be called the Frinton Park Estate. It was to include all the ancillaries - shops, church, railway station, hotel, playing fields and even a tentative site for the new Town Hall. But the Council was not unanimously in favour. At its June meeting in 1935 Mr Lowther Kemp was moved to say that if anybody could suggest land more suitable for a playingfield than the Frinton Park estate, he would be glad to hear of it. It might be said that some people did not want a playing field, but they had to look ahead, and in time it would be in the centre of a built-up area. Councillor Russell Roberts was against it, saying that there were some who thought the playing field a mistake. They also thought the Town Hall site was a mistake. They were in too great a hurry to get these sites. There were open spaces not likely to be filled for a long time. These were prophetic words in that the estate was never completed, and within 40 years the centre of the enlarged area of local government had moved over to Tendring. By November, however, the Council agreed that work on the playing field should be done in stages, with the football pitch top of the list, to be ready for the 1936-7 season.

Meanwhile the Company, with high hopes, sent out an expensively-produced brochure proclaiming, "Frinton Park - a seaside township the like of which has never been seen before in England ... You could be afloat every evening the whole summer through - not just at occasional and always hurried weekends." The focus of the estate was to be a grand 100-bedroom hotel with a great, curving façade overlooking the sea. Even as the brochure was sent on its optimistic way some fifty houses had been put in hand. The shopping centre was to be based in the area of Pedlars Wood. All these plans were subject to the supervision of the innovative architect, Oliver Hill.

But, even though the houses which were built are said to be the largest single collection of 'thirties-style houses in Britain, they still number hardly more than 40. Within a year the Company's cash had run out and buyers were not forthcoming in the expected flood. The ultra-modern, flat-roofed, dazzling white houses cost too much for the conservative, well-breeched but 'careful' clients. The story is summed up in the *Essex Chronicle*, reporting on "... the compulsory liquidation of Maximus Constructions (Limited), agents, builders and contractors ..." A summary of the Company's Statement of Affairs showed liabilities of £7,840 and assets of £4,227. It had been registered on 14th December, 1934, promoted by Dudley Sangster. Its first objective was to take over the business of Frinton Park Estates Ltd which had built some houses before its funds ran out. Under the contract nine houses had been built and 13 houses and four shops partly built. The paper concludes: "Sangster states that difficulty was experienced in selling the houses. The Company found itself in financial difficulties and instructions had to be given to cease work. Sangster attributes the Company's failure to underestimating the contract prices charged to the Estate Company, and, the inability to find purchasers for the houses."

Over fifty years later, in 1990, Councillor Win Shelton was quoted on her view of the estate: "They are a beautiful, unique complex of buildings and we have always thought very highly of that part of Frinton." A plan of the estate, beautifully executed, can be seen in a most unusual form and place. It is laid out in mosaic as the floor of the living room of the Round House. built to serve as the estate office on the corner of Waltham Way and the sea front. Poole Pottery produced the tesserae and Clifford Ellis prepared the plan. Let Rachel Baldwin have the last word. "For today's student of architecture, a stroll around the former Frinton Park Estate is still an education, even though some of the houses have since undergone major alterations and others have been replaced altogether. Waltham Way and Graces Walk, just off the sea front, have the greatest concentration of these modern houses." The estate has now been designated a conservation area.

Time marched on; the Jubilee of the reign of George V, on 6th May, 1935, was celebrated in style with the crowning of a Jubilee Queen, Dorothy Nunnerley, who, with her maids of honour were seated in a decorated car to head the carnival procession from Central Avenue down to the Albion breakwater at Walton where Father Neptune, in full fig, came in from the sea to join the celebrations. The procession included not only decorated vehicles but also adults and children in fancy dress, the latter taking part in races on the greensward in the afternoon.

They had their own celebration tea, while the old people were similarly entertained. Everybody was invited to a carnival dance in the evening. The permanent memorial was to be a sports pavilion on the Recreation Ground. A special Sunday service in the Parish Hall finished off the celebrations.

There was more fun and games in June when those irrepressible Frinton Young Britons went to the Ocean Theatre at Clacton to put on a show in aid of the Clacton Hospital. Those participating included that Beauty Queen Dorothy Nunnerley and her good friend, Mona Darvell, whose memories we have quoted. In September there was another occasion for celebration. The completion of the Free Church was marked by a thanksgiving service when the new entrance was opened with a golden key. The clock in the tower had been given by Alderman Mathews in memory of his mother and father and the rose window was the gift of Mr and Mrs Parkinson.

The tragic report of an air disaster gives, incidentally, a picture of the kind of people who, through the 'thirties, were making Frinton their home. In March Mrs Ursula Horseman was a victim of the crash of the Imperial Airways flying boat

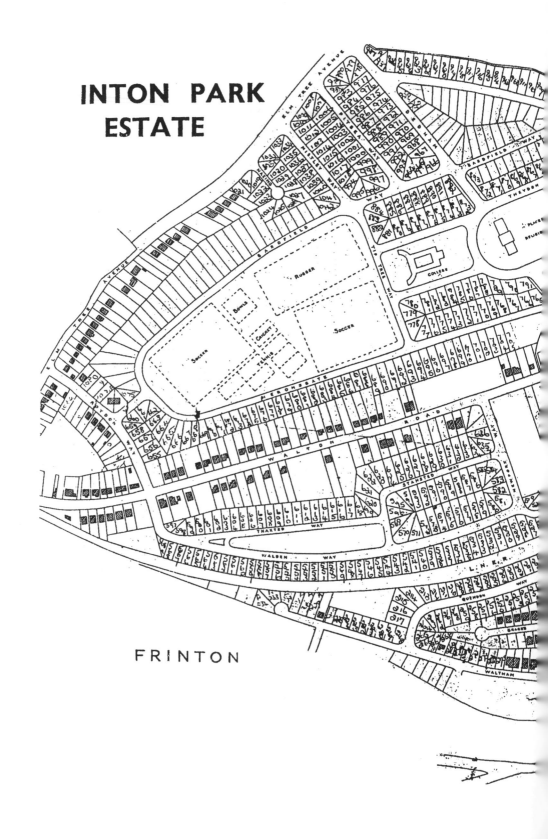

INTON PARK
ESTATE

FRINTON

GREENSWARD

SEA

ESTATE
OFFICE

City of Khartoum at the entrance to Alexandria Harbour. Her husband was a cotton magnate at Cawnpore. They and their four children had a house in Frinton from which he had flown back to Cawnpore the previous year and she was expected to join him in the New Year. Her death, so unexpected, was much felt in Frinton for she was a popular member of golf and tennis clubs and was herself a capable pilot of her own plane.

The agents for Frinton Park Estate were still optimistic in January, 1936. They sent a letter to the Council asking that an early start be made on the construction of the new road between Frinton Esplanade and The Leas on their estate because it was hoped that 30 houses would be completed by the end of the month. When that company collapsed it brought others tumbling with it. Take one example: Mrs Isobel Daniels, baker and café proprietress, was running the Casino restaurant on the Esplanade; saw the new development as a chance for expansion and set up as a baker and cafe called 'Isobel' in Central Avenue. The new houses did not come, nobody called for cakes, her whole business went bankrupt for £765.5s.1d. at the beginning of 1936.

Frinton, however, carried on, some residents being pleased that the feared spread of 'modern' architecture out into the old fields had been halted. The attraction of the place for 'trippers' was causing concern. The Golf Club sent in a letter to the Council on the increasing parking of cars on the Esplanade: "...it seriously spoils the amenities of Frinton, and has a prejudicial effect on the minds of prospective residents and visitors." The Council meeting in February, 1936, decided that a ban would not be appropriate; that the best way forward was "more supervision and control." It sparked a discussion of the general behaviour of visitors on the greensward and the beach which resulted in the suggestion that the number of beach inspectors should be increased from two to four. But that brought, in its turn, a letter from two estate agents saying that visitors proposing to rent beach huts had been very annoyed by the beach inspectors' close questioning. "The visitors said they would not return until it was stopped."

The last county directory ever to be published, in 1937, has a long entry for Frinton, but most of the historical information simply repeats that of earlier editions. It does show Mr W Lowther Kemp, Chairman of the former Frinton Urban District Council still serving his community faithfully as a councillor of the Frinton and Walton council, along with another old-timer, C W Tagg.

Despite plans over the previous years for a new Council House the old one in Old Road still served as their headquarters. Some 215 private residents are entered in the directory. They would not have been the total number of Frinton householders but rather the 'upper crust'. The commercial section contains 114 names of businesses and services, evidence of the growth of the town. Another sign of that burgeoning importance is the entry of Woolworth's shop in Connaught Avenue - a very modern development, for it had not been entered in the 1933 edition. Yet such was the select nature of the town that Woolworth's pulled out in despair.

There were many people in the higher levels of government who had houses in Frinton for their summer relaxation and weekend breaks from the office. Industrial and manufacturing moguls kept up large houses for the same reasons and for the entertainment of important clients from all around the globe. They all knew what a threatening storm was looming from as early as 1933, but ordinary life still had to be lived in Frinton. The council meeting of October, 1936, was busy with the details of grants for and the draining of the land which would form the Frinton Park Estate Playing Field. The clouds of war were obscured by the "... huge clouds of smoke", as the *Daily Mirror* reported, which rose from Mummery's shop in Connaught Avenue as it burned down in July, 1936. They were seen from Clacton on the one hand and Walton on the other.

In February, 1938, the town was attacked once again by its old enemy, the sea, with a raging wind behind it. All the bathing huts for half a mile from the Holland-on-Sea end of the promenade were swept away. Some of them could be seen tossing on the deep like capsized Noah's arks, but those huts built out on piles over the beach were completely broken up into matchwood and carried far out to sea on the receding tide. Local fishermen suffered most, many of their huts, containing a lot of their working gear, were smashed up and washed away. With them went several boats which had been pulled high up on the beach.

In this year, too, the town lost a good and influential friend when Sir Charles Batho died. A ship store and export merchant, he owned Summit House in Second Avenue. To be invited to it was the local equivalent of a royal summons. He made himself available for all manner of 'openings' and garden parties. Another death to make aa impact in Frinton's story was that of William W Race on 28th January, 1939, aged 81. This north-country man spent the last 34 years of his life in the town, working in partnership with the predeceased J W Scott, as farmers, dairymen, coal agents and livery stables, with farms at Kirby Cross and Frinton, and with offices in Connaught Avenue. Ursula Bloom was an enthusiastic traveller by Race and Scott private hire 'buses.

From as early as this Frinton was being considered as a suitable place for the reception of refugees in time of war. The Council decided to await a survey of households by a government agency to assess the accommodation available, but at the same time to make representations to the Minister of Health that their district was not suitable for such refugees. They were to be proved right.

This general feeling of Frinton's exclusivity was demonstrated in the following April when councillors were told of the County Council's bye-laws dealing with "wireless loudspeakers and gramophones". One worthy alderman wanted to know if they applied to "loudspeakers that career about the District". He said there had been many complaints. The Chairman, G C Russell Roberts, said, "It's not the

Mummery & Harris fire (*postcard loaned by Mr M Herbert*)
Fire engine in Connaught Avenue, 1935. Ringing the bell is Mr F Philpot.

sort of thing we want here. It is spoiling the amenities of the district." The Alderman backed him up: "It lowers the tone of the place."

By July the outbreak of war with Germany was not just anticipated, it was expected daily. Frinton was involved in a big A.R.P. 'practice' based on Colchester, and there were long waiting lists for recruitment to the Territorial forces. Within a fortnight the local A.R.P. rehearsal had been extended to a 'black-out' and an air raid precaution exercise over the whole of South-East England. One day before the declaration of war the local paper announced on 2nd September, "INTERNATIONAL CRISIS - Hitler broadcasts he has no other choice but to meet force with force."

Within a week an evacuation scheme had been introduced whereby Frinton was to help accommodate people from the areas under more immediate threat from German attack by air or sea. Several trains took thousands of bewildered evacuees to Clacton from where buses took children and some mothers to areas like Frinton and Walton. Yet it was a fact that, within six weeks, of 3,000 evacuees to the Tendring area, one third had returned home. But there were still many evacuees in Frinton and Walton when the District Council announced the end of its local "war emergency working arrangements."

When the shouting stopped and the shooting started after some months of the 'phoney war' events accelerated. The Ministry of Health decided in May, 1940, that all schoolchildren in areas on the Essex coast should be moved to new billets in Glamorgan, Monmouthshire and neighbouring counties by special trains clear across the country. The first to go were the 700 children already evacuated from their Edmonton homes to Clacton, Walton and Frinton. Next month Frinton was declared part of the 'defence area' stretching from the Wash to Rye in Sussex. The Regional Civil Defence Commissioner had the power to control all movement of civilians in the area.

It all happened during July, 1940. After midnight on the 9th no private car could use any road within five miles of Frinton unless the driver had an essential user's permit. From the 12th all small craft had to be removed from the beach and stored inland. On the 28th the curfew was introduced. Everyone had to be off the streets from one hour after sunset until one hour before sunrise. Frintonians were encouraged to move inland if it was at all possible. Churchill's internal memorandum of 5th stated: "Clear instructions should now be issued about the people living in the threatened [by invasion] coastal zones. They should be encouraged as much as possible to depart voluntarily ... Those who wish to stay, or can find nowhere to go on their own, should be told that if invasion impact occurs in their town or village on the coast they will not be able to leave till the battle is over ..." By mid-July half the population of Frinton had moved inland. The government responded by freeing them from all responsibility for rents, rates and other charges for public services at their Frinton address.

Beach Hotel, 1930. Destroyed during WWII (*photograph loaned by Mr M Herbert*)
Corner of the Esplanade and Eton Road damaged by sea-mine, 17th November, 1941.

By August Frinton was almost a ghost town. Nobody other than the military or a police officer in uniform was allowed upon the beach, and so many houses had been left vacant that they were at grave risk from housebreakers. Two Gunners who broke into W J Kohring's house, The Haven, Elm Tree Avenue in August were apprehended by PC Theobald in another garden. The seriousness of the situation had been graphically demonstrated as early as 3rd July when German planes dropped 27 high explosive bombs. Mercifully they landed on the golf course and no-one was hurt. Another attack the same month was similarly and mercifully ineffective. On October 26th, 1940, the *East Essex Gazette* got round the censor's ban on identifying victims of bombing by reporting "Bombs fell in the gardens of unoccupied houses in a small east coast resort on Sunday morning, and not even a window was broken ... the fourth was in the gardens of "Hollywood" the property of Mr T Cannon-Brooks..." - and this gentleman is shown in the 1937 county directory as residing at Frinton, albeit in a house of another name.

On 18th January, 1941, it was-reported that no less than 119 Essex churches had been damaged by enemy action since air raids began and four of them had been completely destroyed. At the same time soldiers of the 8th Battalion were down on the beach in the cold of winter erecting the steel scaffolding 'barrier' which it was hoped would frustrate German attempts at landing an invasion force. That same year, as some old residents may remember, a Swedish ship, the *Belgia* came ashore, on fire, on that same beach. The fire was put out, but it took tugs several days to get her clear of the shallows again, ready for towing to Harwich. All through the operation the Frinton and Walton lifeboat, the *E. M. E. D.* gave all the assistance it could.

In August, 1942, the Council refused another application by Eastern National to be allowed to run a bus service right into town. It is surprising just how many people had returned to Frinton by this time. The authorities had to adopt a new contingency plan - compulsory evacuation of all the east coast towns was to be put in hand immediately invasion was shown to be imminent by reconnaissance planes on regular patrol. The ban on new residences being taken up in Frinton remained in force throughout 1943. And through this year, too, hit-and-run bombing continued. On 14th March six Focke-Wulf 109's came roaring in at sea level. In May they paid another visit, causing the paper to say, in the style approved by the Censor that "two neighbouring East Coast towns were attacked. "This is the worst raid the district has known, although sneak raiders are expected, and come, very often." Twelve Focke-Wulfs dropped a spread of bombs which killed five people, injured many more, destroyed the Catholic Church and demolished the Beach Hotel. Another casualty of the senseless destruction was The Den, Second Avenue, where Ernest Kingsman, the owner of Clacton Pier and the *Laguna Belle* had lived with his wife until his death just a year before.

Yet Frinton continued to answer the challenge and keep up its spirits. In July, 1943, the Frinton and Walton Urban District area beat the national record for national savings in the recent "Wings for Victory" week. They achieved an average of £53. 19s. 10d. invested in National Savings per head of population, beating champion Knaresborough's effort by £1 14s. 1d.

The strangest of coincidences occurred when the Beach Hotel received a direct hit in 1943. From the total ruin there was picked the hotel register, and in it could be read the signature of Joachim von Ribbentrop, Hitler's close advisor, who had spent a holiday in Frinton before the war.

Jeremy Russell, in his excellent booklet, *100 years of Frinton's railway*, taking the story down to 1988, shows a sketch which includes three points of real Frinton history - the early semaphore signal, the old water tank high on its stilts and the concrete blockhouse which still survived at the east end of the down platform; one of the few surviving strong points, manned by the Home Guard, which would have given 'Jerry' a hard time if he had dared to invade.

The war with Germany ended on 3rd May, 1945. Frinton had survived over five years of misery, despite food shortages and daily expectation of injury or death from ruthless yet pointless enemy air attacks. There were at least two hundred incidents of damage caused by bombs and rockets. On one night, 14th February, 1944, it has been estimated that a thousand incendiary bombs and 30 tons of high explosive bombs were dropped on the town and its environs. As a result 128 houses wore entirely destroyed, 37 people were killed and some 300 inhabitants were injured.

Suddenly it was peaceful every day in Frinton, loved ones could come back, from evacuation, from war work, from all the services. Soon Frinton was bustling again - and there was so much to do in rebuilding, clearing mines from cliffs and beaches and planning a programme for a new era in Frinton's history.

CHAPTER 10 - FRINTON RESURGENT

There was so much to do in the aftermath of the war in Europe before Frinton could take its place once again as the Queen of peaceful British holiday resorts. First the former inhabitants had to be gathered in from their temporary evacuation. On 11th May, 1945, free travel vouchers and special trains and coaches where necessary brought mothers and children home again. In the *Essex County Standard*, they read of the shower of V1 pilotless planes which were shot down over the region between 16th September, 1944, and 29th March, 1945. These flying bombs, aimed in the direction of London, flew down the coast in a pre-set corridor, to be picked off by the R.A.F., who claimed 76 destroyed, and the Walton and Clacton gun batteries which downed another 30. Many were brought down over the sea.

The wreckage and rubble of bombed houses was still lying about, but men were trickling back from the services to take up work as builders, in the public utilities, and so on. There was a lot of frustration over the slow rate of rebuilding and the new houses yet to be built by the Council. But in 1946 one of the most sensational news stories was that bananas were back! It happened in February when William Smith Ltd. in Colchester had a delivery of 2,040 bunches; enough, said Mr. Smith, "to supply every person in possession of an R.B. 2 or R.B. 4 ration book with one pound per head." They were definitely not for sale to adults - and after five years absence there were many children who had never seen one before. Parents queued up for hours to give them this exciting new eating experience.

The most important work as far as parents and children were concerned had been to put in hand before the cessation of hostilities, culminating in the report in May, 1946, that "'The beach and pipe minefields laid in large areas of Essex throughout the war are now practically cleared." But there were still tragic events as in that very month when 67-year-old Council worker Herbert Kerridge was killed by a mine which exploded as he and his workmates were clearing away barbed wire from the steps down the cliff near Walton pier.

The war had been over for a year but not a Council house had been put in hand because of delay at the Ministry of Health in organising its scheme of issuing licences over the whole district. In face of the adverse criticism from its townsfolk the Council sent a deputation to the Ministry seeking clarification of the delay. At the same time the Chairman was invited to join another deputation - to the Chief General Manager of the London and North-Eastern Railway to place before him a complaint concerning "... the present unsatisfactory train service to the coast towns." Some people were also against the forward-looking Frinton Amenities Committee of the Council in its efforts to introduce car parking areas, in particular the splendid modern amenity of free parking all along the front on the Greensward side. Councillor C W Hayne declared at the December, 1946, Council meeting that they were "... selling the birthright of the Frinton people." He thought the parking of 559 cars along the front was ridiculous - it was just offering the place as a tripper's paradise. He was backed by J W Eagle who said that the proposal was just perpetuating a nuisance. "In two or three years' time, when more cars are on the road, you will find yourself in such a muddle that you will not be able to get out of it."

History has proved Councillor H F Barker right when he said, "One day this town must provide a car park. Why on earth delay?" By 7 votes to 5 it was agreed that the Esplanade and Connaught Avenue would be the subject of a parking scheme.

There were other signs that things were getting back to normal. On 7th January, 1947, the Conservatives revived their branch association at a meeting in the Empire Hall. The weather was so bad that many of the old supporters like Mrs C A Cooper could not go. Though Mrs Cooper was ill at the time she was elected President in her absence - a tribute to her many years of service to the cause. The Chairman also reminded the meeting that since its last annual meeting before the war the Branch had lost its greatest benefactor and friend when death carried off Ernest Moy. The month ended with very low temperatures, and blizzards of snow which brought electricity cuts and total failures. At the end of March the weather was still hitting the headlines as a post-war problem: "Gale and havoc in wild week-end," said the local paper. At the same time it was announced that Frinton and Walton U.D.C. area had been given permission for the erection of 30 houses, council and private, through this year. The Council spoke out to complain that it would be 1948 before they could, wade through the paperwork and by then local builders would be going bankrupt.

Frinton traders had high hopes as more cars came on to the roads and trains and coaches were running better services on holidays; but the year was dis-appointing; gales swept the coast and the customers stayed at home. Just as well, from one councillor's point of view. He pointed out that the Greensward was a 'disgrace', still covered with barbed wire and other wartime detritus. The Surveyor said it was in hand but would not be cleared before next year. The Tennis Club was really back in business with a tournament in July and pictures of the international stars taking part appeared. By October though, there was still no action on the housing front and a second deputation waited on the Minister, pointing out that there were 400 people on the housing waiting list and not one new house had been started since the end of the war. Frinton and Walton was the only local council with such a dismal record. The problem seemed to hinge on the fact that the Ministry considered that prices in tenders by builders were much too high. It was obvious that the special nature of the area, and the value of houses erected there before the war, had not been taken into account.

The difficulty of finding accommodation for a policeman led to further difficulties and a report in the local paper: "Frinton, the town without a policeman, is demanding 'proper police protection' for householders and shopkeepers". The Council protested in a letter to the Joint Standing Committee. It had been without a policeman in Frinton for a very considerable time, even though it qualified for the provision of two. With new building held up for so long there was little chance of finding a suitable houses or houses in the near future. One councillor hoped the papers would not give too much publicity to their plight, for it could attract burglars to Frinton. "It's all right", said the Chairman, "We have police protection even if we don't have a policeman living here." At last, in May, Frinton having been allowed to start at last on its first six houses, in Witton Wood Road, was given the go-ahead on a further eight of the 30 permitted.

The news that the arrangement of local government areas was under review brought further alarm and despondency. It seemed possible that Frinton and Walton would be absorbed into a much large area running from the border of Brightlingsea practically up to Harwich and running inland to include Great Bentley and Thorpe-le-Soken. That reorganisation came to nothing and was replaced by another scheme years later, but there was nothing tentative about the nationalisation of the electricity industry from 1st April, 1948. Even here, though, there was qualified improvement, for by the end of the year Frinton was still on D.C. Electricity and the state-owned industry could give no assurance of an early prospect of change to the much-to-be-preferred A.C. (Alternating Current) supply. It was good news for council workers and bad news for the ratepayers when it was announced that the wages of council workmen were to be increased by 6s. (30p) a week, and their hours reduced to 44 a week without detriment. The Frinton and Walton Urban District Council was much concerned because it reckoned that the award would cost some £2,000 a year and nothing had been allowed in the Council budget for such an unforeseen increase. The Chairman said he would like the ratepayers to know that this could be the reason that some of the work expected to be done was not carried out.

Frinton's big houses, so fashionable before the war when labour was cheap, were becoming more of a liability rather than a status symbol for many of the older inhabitants. Old folk, or their executors, were looking for a solution, and came up with the idea of conversion into flats. That did not go down well with their neighbours. Miss Lea had lived in Eastry, a 16-roomed house in Third Avenue before the war. Now she wanted to convert it, at a cost of £1,800 into flats 'for the same type of person who already, or in pre-war days, lived in that area of Frinton'. Her solicitor made a moot point: "We are living in a changing world. There are a large number of these big houses in Frinton, and I am going to suggest that the time is coming when it will be increasingly difficult to find occupiers for large houses." Even the Frinton estate agent A S Tomkins said he saw no future in this type of property as a private residence. The Council Chairman gave his opinion - "Frinton is a model of town planning throughout the country. The local authority is very loth to have its amenities spoilt."

Not surprisingly, then, in March Frinton and Walton Council strongly opposed the County Council's plan for an 'aged persons' hostel' at the Willows, "situated between two high-class hotels and near other large and superior properties."

The Chairman, Mr H A Girt, was heard to say, "There is nothing in Frinton to attract these old people except sitting down and watching the sea." At this time the newspaper looked back fifty years to March, 1899, and reminded its readers of what happened regularly before Frinton got its Sea Defences Act of 1903: "During the past week one of the largest landslips took place at Frinton-on-Sea nearly opposite the Queen's Hotel and along the frontage of the football ground for a distance of over 200 feet in length, this being the third of a series of large slips ... during the past 12 months within about a mile's walk of Frinton. When such pieces as 150 feet square of land - which is the measurement of one piece fallen - go at a time, the greensward is materially diminished."

On 4th March, 1949, the storm was just as severe. The gale blew the high tide even higher and washed away a hundred bathing huts on the Frinton and Walton promenades.

Another application for permission to convert a house, the Brown House, in Second Avenue was leased by the Council. The solicitor for the applicant made the telling observation that "Frinton is tending to become more of a residential town." The number of flats in the town has vastly increased, and some of the big old houses have been demolished to make way for a number of smaller, more easily managed houses to be lived in annually rather than just for the 'season' which has now vanished as the jumbo-jets take everybody to guaranteed warmth and sunshine. The number of large houses taken over as retirement homes and nursing homes indicates that the Council had to bow to the changing circumstances.

Another council policy was firmly upheld when Frinton Young Conservatives asked if they might be allowed to hold a fête on the Greensward in July, 1949. The Council responded "... it is their practice not to permit use of the Greensward for such purposes to political organisations." Sport was being catered for as well as ever, it was before the war. The town's cricket team had good news and bad in this '49 season. Late in June, playing against the combined talent of Colchester and East Essex they found themselves needing 148 runs to win, tea already taken, and just 110 minutes left. They made it, with five minutes to spare and six wickets in hand, through the great innings, 93 not out, by opening batsman, Bill Chambers. The bad news was the burning down of their pavilion while they were out on the field, during a match with Brunswick. They, and the batsmen, had to sprint in to rescue their clothes and personal belongings. Frinton Fire Brigade, under SO Baker, had to run hose over half a mile to the hydrant in First Avenue. Sad to say all the club's records and photographs since 1900 were completely destroyed. There was no story of sabotage behind it - just an over-heated oil stove. 'Tray' Crinter, the President, immediately launched an appeal fund.

In July several famous Wimbledon stars came to Frinton to take part in their tournament, including the Australian, G E Brown, the Swede, S Laftman, the Chinese, W Choy, and the American, Mrs P C Todd, as well as their own local junior champion, J A T Horn. What the older, more conservative townsfolk thought of the Harrow Car Club rally along the greensward, with cocktails at 6.30 and dancing into the night at the Grand Hotel was not disclosed in press reports.

But they would have felt better for the announcement that "A start will soon be made on the erection of 59 Police houses in the 1949-50 programme for Essex ... two at Frinton cost £3,850." The two at Thorpe-le-Soken cost around £500 less.

Under the novel headline of FRINTON OBJECTS TO THE HOUSE OF CONSECRATED FUN the local paper told how the Council, unwittingly, had given permission for the establishment at the 20-roomed Kelvin House in Fourth Avenue of a Christian Youth Holiday Centre. The idea was put forward by Maurice Rowlandson who lived in the town at Appletrees. He had seen this kind of happy Christianity in action in the U.S.A. and wanted to serve English youth in the same way. He brought out a brochure which talked of waking the Centre at 7.30 a.m. by 'a xylophone gong' and continuing with stirring choral music. Later in the day there would be 'much sanctified humour and consecrated fun ... where laughter and song breaks the quiet of the evening air.' It seemed harmless enough but 58 owners of property in the vicinity were sufficiently concerned to register their objection. One old inhabitant said: "After hearing of the loudspeakers and the singing, it came to my mind that this would be a miniature Butlin's with a Christian flavour. Should these people succeed in bringing the project to fruition, 180 other properties on the Cooper estate would depreciate in value by as much as £100,000. Mr Rowlandson said all the windows would be closed while the Young Christians enjoyed themselves. Three weeks later, on 14th October, 1949, the official arbitrator gave his verdict against the holiday centre and the local paper provided the epitaph - "No consecrated fun." At the same time the District Council was asked to receive a deputation from the Chamber of Commerce to discuss possible improvements to Frinton, for inhabitants and visitors alike. With wartime restrictions on supplies of all kinds now being relaxed buildings could be put in hand and businesses installed within them to meet the demand for further shops and services.

Frinton's fierce independence was demonstrated once again at the beginning of 1950. There had been much talk and negotiation for a joint celebration of the forthcoming Festival of Britain by towns and villages in north Essex, but Frinton finally decided it would opt out and do its own thing.

It was very annoyed, too, when the Ministry of Food decided that Frinton Food Office would be degraded to a mere sub-office of Colchester from where staff would be sent out on certain days to administer unto Frinton folk and their holiday guests. Since no less than 22,000 emergency ration cards had been issued through the previous year, mostly at peak holiday time, it did seem that an independent office was justified.

That first month of the new year saw another ancient tradition broken. For the first time in Frinton's history buses were allowed to enter those hallowed tree-lined avenues 'inside the gates' to pick up passengers. There had been some buses allowed to pass over the level crossing and through the gates before but they had only been in the course of special Sunday evening tours, and they were not allowed to stop once inside those gates. This new facility did not last long - it was simply because all trains which would have passed through the station were cancelled while the old bridge at Kirby Cross was being repaired.

It happened on Sunday, 8th January, 1950. The railmen worked Saturday night, all day Sunday and again through the night so that the first regular train crossed the bridge again at 5 a.m. on Monday morning.

There was always a sense of rivalry between the two major members of the Frinton and Walton Urban District Council until at last, in 1974, the authority was enlarged to include a much wider swathe of northeast Essex as the new Tendring District of local government. Then the greatest good for the greatest number made the little squabbles of the two resorts look as light-hearted as they should do. So we can now smile at the report on 2nd February, 1950, that "the usual peace and quiet of the Council Chamber" were disturbed by an argument over whether Walton should have £450 or £350 for advertising in the coming year. Mr H A Girt favoured the smaller sum: "... after all, dear little Walton is only a small watering village. You haven't much attraction down here for all these visitors to come to ... I assure the people of Walton that the fat plutocrats of Frinton are not always going to be bled in keeping Walton going ..." he lost the day however and peace was restored!

This year there was some looking back and reminiscence as the old founding fathers of Frinton's prosperity took their last journey through the church porch. Frank T Neale, who died in February, aged 77, was the founder of F T Neale and Sons, the Connaught Avenue drapers and outfitters, back in 1908.

When the effects of Dr G Aldridge were sold at his house, 'Hurstlyn' in Fourth Avenue some comparisons could be made with the furniture of other Frintonians of note. His gas cooker went for £14.10s., his grandfather clock for £17, his Rinnerman piano for £26, and that status symbol, the 1937, Austin Goodwood 16 h.p. car attracted a bid of £310.

One man, who had started business as an estate agent in partnership with his father in Frinton in 1919, full of confidence and no little hope was C W Hayne of Wilsley, Third Avenue. But here he was, some forty years later, facing trial at the Quarter Sessions on seven charges of fraudulently converting clients' money to the tune of £1,900. For fifteen years he had been on the Urban District Council. His counsel described him as a man 'virtually ruined by the war'.

And so the year of 1950 meandered to a close with Frinton looking forward to another season of holidaymakers in hotels and private houses - opening them for 'the season' - but for how much longer? The trippers, by cars, in their thousands, were beginning to weigh down the see-saw of Frinton's selectivity to the end where ordinary folk, without wealth or title, looking for a peaceful place in which to relax away from the noise and the vulgarities of the last half of the twentieth century, found that Frinton filled the bill.

There are so many still alive in Frinton today who have lived through this period that a history projected beyond 1950 would be an affront to their own memories and recollections of events. So we close this book of Frinton, with thanks to all those kind people who helped us on our way.

The beach in the mid-fifties (photograph loaned by Mr M Herbert)

The Cedars, 1896 (loaned by Mrs T Milwain)

Ocean View, 1906 (postcard loaned by Mr M Herbert)

BIBLIOGRAPHY

Benham, William Gurney. Essex sokens

Boyden, Peter B. Frinton before the Stuarts; the story of pre-historic and mediæval Frinton. Walton Record Office, 1978

Boyden, Peter B. The growth of Frinton; 1600-1914. Walton Record Office, 1973

Cuttle, George, *compiler*. Newscuttings on poor law and local government.

Dewes, Simon. Essex schooldays. Hutchinson, 1960

Ford, Peter. Tendring peninsula. Ian Henry, 1988

Walker, Kenneth. Martello Towers and the defence of N.E.Essex in the Napoleonic War. Reprinted from the *Essex Review*, Vol. XLVII, October, 1938.

Watson, J Yelloly. The Tendring Hundred in the olden time. 2nd ed. Benham & Harrison, 1878

Whitaker, William. The geology of the eastern end of Essex (Walton Naze and Harwich). Memoirs of the Geological Survey, HMSO, 1877

White, Philip *and* White, Colin. Frinton and its parish churches. Part 1: Historical Frinton parish church, 1979.

Whybrew, Derick. The story of Frinton Free Church, 1990.

Station Road, 1904 (postcard loaned by Mrs T Milwain)

Abergavenny, Marquis of 79
Abyssinia, Emperor of 79
Ady, Archdeacon 41-3
Aldridge, Dr G 128
Alston, Edward 13
Alston, Pennings 13
Anderson, Frank 73
Annis, Dr 22
Ashlyns Road 71,78-9
Ashmall, Charles 75
Avery, Joseph 16-17
Bacon, Lionel 20
Bailey, William 58
Baker, Ada 49
Baker, Henry 49
Baker, James 10
Baker, M E F 64
Baker, Robert 10,49
Baker, Samuel 27
Baker, William 19-21
Baker, SO 127
Baldwin, Rachel 62,113
Balls, Guirton 22
Bamber, T M 100,102
Bambridge, Cecil 68
Bangs, Billy 92
Bangs, Percy J 78,104,106,108
Baptist Union 61,100,102
Bare, Gentrey 36
Barker, H F 124
Barnard, Elizabeth 27,30,32,42
Barry, Thomas 7
Bates, Frances 12,64
Batho, Charles 108,118
Battery Point 25
Bawtree, John 42
Beach Hotel 68,121
Beach House Hotel 90,100
Beadle, Frank 23,45-50,52-3,56
Beckett, John 21
Bell, Dr 91
Bellamy, Edward 20-1
Bellamy, Kenny 92
Benham, Gurney 13
Bennett, Arnold 62
Bevington family 64,78
Bing, Viscountess 109
Bird, Thomas 19
Bloom, Ursula 78,85-92,118
Blowers & Cooper 94
Board School 64,73
Bohun, Humphrey 5
Bouchier family 7
Bowes Lyon family 94
Box, Herbert 59
Box, Richard 22
Boyden, Peter B 5,7,9,37,64

Boys Brigade 83
Boys Prep School 73
Brackenbury, Betsy 36
Brackenbury, John & Martha 36
Bradwell on Sea 7
Braithwaite, Lillian 90
Brett, Sarah 33
Bridges, Frederick & Nellie 59
Bright, Jack 94
Brightlingsea 1,125
Bromley, Peter 27,30
Brookman, Billy 90
Brough, Mr & Mrs 106
Brown, A Douglas 102
Brown, G E 127
Brown, I S 34
Brown, Isabella 9
Brown, J Murray 106
Brown, James 46
Brown, William 9
Browne family 32
Bruff, Peter S 1,45,47,49,53,62,73
Brusher, I J 28
Buckmaster, John & Joan 90
Burgess, Jeremia & Penelope 11
Burgess, Dr 91
Burnham, John de 6
Burnham, William de 5
Burrell, Mr 23
Bushell, James 13,17,21
Butcher, John & Caroline 35
Cambridge Road 71
Cannon-Brooks, T 121
Carrington, Benjamin 27
Cary, Joyce 90
Cawston, Barbara 11
Central Avenue 112-4
Chamber of Commerce 127
Chamberlain, Ralph 20
Chamberlayne, Arthur R 64
Chamberleyn, Robert 6-7
Chambers, Bill 126
Charnock, E G 27-8
Children's Special Service Mission 92,97
Chilvers, Mrs E 73
Choy, W 127
Christian Science 91
Christy, Miller 1
Churchill, Randolph 90
Churchill, Winston 78,90
Clacton 1,2,9,10,56
Clark, Andrew 42-4, 83
Clouting, Ada 73
Cockain, Dorothy 20
Cockain, Francis 9,20
Cockayne, Marie 10
Codd, W 36

Colchester 6,10,13,16-7,51
Coller, David 15
Collins, F H 102
Collins, George 73
Conly, J B 109
Connaught, Arthur, Duke of 82
Connaught Avenue 2,15,51,60-2,68,71-3,77-8,81-2,85,94-100,114,118,128
Cook, David 66
Cook, Thomas H 58-9,73
Cooper Mrs C A 94
Cooper, Mrs E 94,106,108,110
Cooper, Gladys 81,90
Cooper, James & Caroline 36
Cooper, John & Jane 36
Cooper, Richard A 87
Cooper, Richard P 62,64,69,71,79,81,87
Cooper, Robert 22
Cooper, Thomas D 27,29,32
Cornwallis, Charles 25
Corser, John L 75
Corten, Nancy 94
Cottenham, Earl of 79
Coxhead, W L 11
Crescent 102
Cricket Club 84,106,126
Crinter, Tray 127
Crombie, William 61
Cross, Robert 33
Culmer, John 20
Cuthbert, W H 75
Cutting, Adery 14
Daly, Eliza 42
Daniels, Daniel 23
Daniels, Isobel 114
Daniels, John & Anna 23
Daniels, John D 32
Darme, David 16
Darvell, Mona 92-100,113
Davies, Daniel 59
Dennis, Sammy 28
Dewes, Simon 81,84
Dillerson, John 33
Dillerson family 33,36
Dillman, Sarah 40
Dive, Mr 40
Dockrell, William R 75,83
Dolling, Mrs R H 102
Donovan, Mr 94
Dovewood, J 6
Dow, Harry 110
Doyley, Officer 18
Dundas, Francis 25
Dunn, Tom 73
Dupont, F 54
Dymock, Humphrey 9
Eagle, J W 109,124

Eastern National 106,121
Ellis, Clifford 113
Elm Tree Avenue 51,121
English, John & Sarah 23
English, Mary 23
English, Boy 22
Eshelby, Edwin 75
Esplanade 68-71,100,113
Esplanade Hotel 90,100
Eton Road 71
Eustace, Earl 13
Evanson, E F C 106
Faiers, Mrs 81
Fairbanks, Douglas 78,98
Farrance, Mary Ann & Lucy 35
Felgate, Alfred 52
Felgate, Robert 39
Fenwick, Councillor 83
Fields, Gracie 97
Fifth Avenue 71,92
Fire Brigade 126
Firmin, Diana 28
Firmin, Eleanor 29,33,52
Firmin, James 28,33
Firmin family 33,36
First Avenue 71,127
Fitch, John 22
Fitton, Henry 7
Fitz Bernard, John 5
Fitz Oger, Michael & Sarah 4
Fitz Oger, Oger & Amy 4
Fitz Richard, Ralph 4
Fitzralph, Richard 5
Flack, William 17
Forthe, Mr 10
Fourth Avenue 2,68,71,75,109,127-8
Fowler, Miss 77
France, William 58
Franklin, Mrs 78
Free Church 60-1,73,85,100,113
Freeman, Robert & Sarah 22-3
Freeman, Samuel 23
Freeman, Widow 22
Freeman, Boy 22
Freemasons 82
Frinton Battery 25
Frinton College 64,73,79,81
Frinton Lodge Hotel 64
Frinton Park Estate 112-118
Frinton U D C 62 68,71-7,85,91,100,105-6
Frinton & Walton U D C 68,109,118,122-3,125-9
Fritha 3
Gallant, Margaret 33
Garrett, Mary 18
Gas & Water Company 77
Geraldine, Queen 79

Gibson, Mary 27
Gilders, Edwin T 69
Gillingham, William G 58-9,62
Girt, Inspector 106
Girt, H A 126,128
Godfrey, Dr 90
Godmanston, Joanna 7
Godmanston, John 6
Godmanston, Phillipa 7,9
Godmanston, William 6,7
Golds, T W 77
Goldsmith, Miss 73
Golf Club 25,62,71-5,78,82,84,106,109,114
Gover, John 11
Graces Walk 112-3
Grand Hotel 64,75,90,127
Grant, Isobel 94
Gray, Mary 20
Gray, Sylvia 94
Great Bentley 125
Great Clacton 23,25,32
Great Holland 10,39-40,47,54,59,69,85,91
Great Horkesley 37
Green, William 28,44,49
Greensward 11,26,62,71,73,77,92,97,100,110,124,126-7
Grieve, Hilda 37,77
Griggs, Young 52
Grimes, Joseph 41-2,45,49-50
Grimston, Edward 9,20
Grimston, Harbottle 9,11,13,20,47
Grimston, Henry 14
Gros, Walter le 5
Hadleigh Road 71,81
Halstead 12
Hanmere, John 9
Harding, Frederick 64
Hardwick, Frances 59
Harman, Arthur H 58
Harman, James 53,58-61
Harman, John A 61,71,77
Harman, Sarah 59
Harold Grove 91
Harold Road 60,64,71,78,91-2
Harris, Robert 22
Harvey, 'Egg' 92
Harvey, Eliza 33
Harvey, Samuel & Sarah 35
Harvey, Mr 40,87
Harvey family 33,36
Harwich 1,25,125
Hawes, Michael 32
Hay, Andrew 25
Hayhoe, William 33,36
Hayne, C W 4,6,109,124,128
Hayne, W 102
Hazard, William 52

Hazel, Theo & Desmond 92
Hearn, Mrs 29
Hector, John 42
Hemmings, William & Mary 36
Hewitt, Mr 22
Hicks, Albert 42
Hicks, Charles 49
Hicks, J T J 47,49
Hicks, Seymour 90
Hicks, T W 11,41,44,102
Hicks family 39,52
Hill, Oliver 112
Hills, Philip 27,29
Hills, Michael 21
Hills, Robert 15,34
Hinsum, Anne 17
Hinsum, James 17,21,23
Hinsum, John 23
Holborough, A M 46-7,50
Holland 6,40
Holland Road 77
Holman, Phyllis 90
Holman, William 12
Home Guard 122
Home for Aged Men & Women 73
Homer, Arnest C 100
Hopkins, Richard 19-20
Horn, J A T 127
Horseman, Ursula 113
Howard, William 35
Huckle, William & Hannah 59
Huckle, Mr 94
Humphrey, Hector 77
Humphrey, Thomas & Sarah 52,59
Hussey, Gilbert 7
Hynd, Geoffrey 7
Innes, William 64,73,79
James, John & Sarah 36
Johnson, A 54
Jones, Mrs 79
Jonson, Ebenezer 22
Joyner, Richard 42,49-50
Joynes, William 102
Junior Imperial League 94
Junior Busy Bee 102
Kemp, W Lowther 104-6,109,112,114
Kerr, Miss M 108
Kerridge, Herbert 123
King, John & Sarah 35
King, John I 75
Kingsbury, John 37
Kingsman, Ernest 121
Kirby, John L 28,34
Kirby Cross 51,128
Kirby Quay 2,109
Kirby Road 71
Kirby-le-Soken 17-8,35,37,39,47,54,64,69,

8,35,37,39,47,54,64,69,104
Knight, Revd 91
Knock, Mr 22
Kohring, W J 121
Laftman, S 127
Laker, Elizabeth 33,35
Langham, Mr 60
Langston, Henry 73
Lawn Tennis Club 64,75,78-9,84,104,106, 124
Lea, Miss 125
Leach, William & Sarah 39
Lee, Simon & Mary 14
Leke, John 9
Levesun 3
Leys, de, family 5
Little Clacton 28,32,44,49
Little Holland 5,13,25,37
Lockwood, Mary Ann 40
Loke, Frances V 28,32,34,37
Longhurst, T J 85,100
Lott, H 52
Luff, Mr 91,94
Luke, Agnes 36
Luke, J V 27,29
Lushington, Charlotte 34,37,44
Lushington, William 26,27,29,31
Lynn, George 20,21
Macdonald, Patrick O 68,73-7,105-6
Malster, Robert 66
Mandeville, Geoffrey de 3,4,13
Mango, Mr 92
Mann, Gother 26
Marci, Rald de 3
Marconi's Wireless Telegraph Training College 73
Marine Parade 58-9
Marine Land & Investment 53-56,64,87
Markham, Henry 106
Marshall, Thomas E 75,91
Martello Tower 26,32
Martin, William 16
Mathews, Alderman 113
Maximus Constructions 110,112-3
Mayhew, Mr 40
McClintock, Revd 91
McGrigor, D B 109
McJannet, Miss M 109
Mead, Phyllis 108
Micklefield, William 29
Moore, Elizabeth 14
Moore, John 25
Mopted, Henry 10
Morant, Philip 12,14,20
Moreton, John 9
Morris, Jack 79
Moy, Ernest J 87,106,124

Muffle, Thomas 14
Mummery's 118
Munson, John 75
Neale, Frank T 128
Newman, Widow 22
Newton, Samuel 22
Nice, Moses 22
Nicholson, Charles 103
Nicholson, S 108
Norden, John 13
Norfod, Geoffrey de 4,5
Nott, John 39
Novello, Ivor 90
Nunnerley, Dorothy 113
Old Road 15,61,68,71-7,82,85,91,94,109, 114
Operatic Society 94
Osborne, Glidden 78
Osgood 3
Oxford Road 71
Oxoe, Thomas 59
Page, R J 62
Parish Council 68
Parkinson, Mr & Mrs 113
Parmenter, Charlotte 33
Parsloe, Frederick B 42
Partridge, Florence 59-60
Passmore, F T 61
Perriment, George & Mary Ann 39
Pertwee, Norman F 78-9
Phillips, John 33,35
Phipps, Charles C 40
Pirton, William 20
Pitt, Archie 97
Plesingho, Stephen de 5
Plymouth Brethren 82,91
Pole Barn Lane 53,71-5,92-7,106
Ponder, Debrah 17
Popperwell family 39,52
Popplewell, Harry 52
Porter, Thomas 10-1,14
Post Office 75,77
Potter, H, & Son 102
Pybus, John 109
Queen's Hotel 54,58,64,71,126
Queens Road 59
Race & Scott 81,100,118
Race, William W 118
Raglan Road 71
Railway Station 39,51-3,58-9,64,75,94,97, 106
Rainald 3
Ram, Elizabeth 17
Ramsey 18
Rand, Sarah 33
Ratcliffe, Barbara & Norma 100
Ratcliffe, Telford 73,100

Red Hills 2
Renelm 3
Resker, Mr 22
Rex, William 40,46
Reynard, E H 32,34,37
Ribbentrop, Joachim von 122
Rice, John 19
Richards, Audrey 92
Rivers family 34,37
Roberts, G C Russell 109,112,118
Robinson, A Douglas 62
Rokell, Geoffrey 6,7
Rokell, John 7
Roman Catholic Church 92,121
Rowland, Samuel & Hannah 36
Rowlandson, Maurice 127
Ruly, Geoffrey de 6
Russell, Jeremy M 51,122
Sadler, Joseph 33
St Mary's 6,11-12,16,24,37,41-3,45-52,54, 56,60,73,102,109
St Osyth 25
Sallows family 34-5
Sandys-Bird, J V 102,105
Sangster, Dudley 112-3
Saunders, Mr 90
Scipper, Thomas 21
Scott, J W 118
Sea Fencibles 25
Second Avenue 71,77,79,87,118,121,126
Selby, Richard 7
Setterfield, Robert G 75
Shadwell, W L 26
Shaw, Gabriel & Elizabeth 20
Shaw, Mrs 81
Shelton, Win 113
Shepherd, Mr 56
Sherell, George & Alice 35
Sichel, Ludwig 75
Skirman's Fee 9,10,13,20,34
Smee, Rosse 59
Smith, A E 104,106
Smith, Eliza 75
Snare, James 36
Snare, William 35
Snell, H W J 106
Snell, Walter 22
Snelling family 91
South Coast Property Investment 112
Southgate, John 59
Spurgeon, Charles H 61
Stanford, C M 69
Station Road see Connaught Avenue
Sterling, Henry 11
Stern, Albert 79
Stokes, Lieutenant 25
Stone, A 44

Stone, Henry 42,45-6,50-1
Stone, Mary Ann 42,49
Stone, Richard 11,12,17-18,21-23,25,27-53, 58,64
Stone, Richard V 40
Stone, Rose J 42,49,51
Stone, William 27,49,51
Stone family 33,35,39
Stony, John 7
Stow, William & Emma 59
Strand, Samuel 17
Stuart, K 81
Sutherwood, George 39,52
Swallow, Joseph 17,21
Tagg, C W 106,109,114
Taylors grocers 77
Tendring 10
Tendring District Council 69,128
Tendring Hundred Waterworks 1,58,69,77
Tendring Rural District 68
Teye, William 11
The Crescent 14
The Leas 77,114
Theedam, Charles 34-5,37
Theedam, Eliza 35
Theobald, PC 121
Third Avenue 69-75,125,129
Thompson, William 32
Thorpe-le-Soken 1,15,21,22,32,77,125
Thurgur, G A 109
Thurston, Joseph 20
Tilbury, Cornelius a 14

Tillet, William 32
Tillingham, Walter of 6
Toby, John 7
Todd, Mrs P C 127
Tomkins, A S 109,125
Tomkins, Homer & Ley 62,69
Travers, Ralph 4,5
Tregoz, Agnes & Petronilla 4
Tricket family 5
Tuke, William 22
Tutthill, Elizabeth 39
Upper Fourth Avenue 69
Upper Third Avenue 69
Victoria Terrace 59
Vidler, Eliza 59
Volunteer Lifeboat Society 66,68
Voysey, Charles F A 77
Wade, Edward 59
Wadsman, Arnest 73
Wales, Edward, Prince of 78,91
Walker, Christiana 9
Walker, Henry 9
Walker, Kenneth 26,40
Walters, Abraham 10
Waltham Way 77,104,112-3
Walton 1,3,6,18-9,37,51,56,58
Warren, Bentley 28
Warren, Elizabeth 13,20
Warren, Jeremiah 13,20
Warren, Joan 13,17
Warren, Robert 17
Warren, Thomas 13,20

Warren family 12,20
Watson, Jeremy 20
Watts, Christian 33
Weatherhead, H 75
Webb, Samuel 42
Webster, William 75
Weslyan Methodist Chapel 82
West, Abel 64
Whitaker, William 1
White, P & C 14
White, William 34
White House Hotel 78,108
Whitmore, Richard 9
Whitton Wood Lane 92,104,110,125
Whybrow, Derek 100
Wilkinson, S H 61,85,102
Willan, Richard 23
Wilmer, Foxy & Leslie 92
Wilson, Peter 64
Winchester Road 71
Wollmer, Thomas 11
Womack, Thomas & Emma 59
Women's Institute 108-9
Woodroffe, C 37
Woods, Galin 59
Woodstock, Thomas of 7
Wreathall, R T 54
York, Frederick, Duke of 25
Young, Mr 58
Young Britons 94,108,110,113
Young Conservatives 126
Zog, King 79

Second World War fortifications (photograph loaned by Mr M W Herbert)

Sandy Hook, mid-thirties (postcard loaned by Mr M Herbert)

Beach below the Grand Hotel, 1930s (postcard loaned by Mr M Herbert)